I0813310

"In an American culture that disapproves of Christianity, strategies for ministry that attempt to be 'relevant' to the culture are bound to fail. Senkbeil and Woodford help us see that this cultural moment merely highlights what has always been true: that clinging to the Word of Christ is not only the God-given means of salvation but the Spirit-given heart of the life of the church in its mission to the world. This little book, itself full of the Word of Christ, may help free pastors to cling to the Word rather than grope for strategies of relevance."

—**PHILLIP CARY**, professor of philosophy and scholar-in-residence at the Templeton Honors College, Eastern University, Philadelphia; author of *Good News for Anxious Christians* and *The Meaning of Protestant Theology*

"Are you ready for a breath of fresh air amid the cacophony of voices that have dominated the landscape of the church for decades? Are you ready for a biblical framework amid the duplicitous programs that have failed to contextualize the gospel for decades? If so, this delightful little book is for you. With the Acts of the Apostles as our compass, Drs. Senkbeil and Woodford keep church and society in their rightful place. There is much here for the church to ponder—not only how we think and speak theologically, but more importantly how the church lives and breathes the mission given her at this very time. Refreshing."

—**BART DAY,** president and CEO, Lutheran Church Extension Fund (LCEF)

"Few things are better for the soul than reading Lutherans on the power of God's word. Senkbeil and Woodford's call to pastors and churches to give priority to the living word of the risen Christ in their ministries and liturgies is timely and welcome. Anyone who reads this book will walk away with renewed faith in the gospel, revived commitment to the church, and restored confidence in the Spirit of God rather than the spirit of the age."

—**BRAD EAST,** associate professor of theology, Abilene Christian University, Texas; author of *The Church: A Guide to the People of God*

"One consequence of living in a technique-obsessed age that is always chasing fads and 'innovation' is that it is easy to forget basics. Imagine a chef who has mastered an elaborate weird new cooking technique but has forgotten basic knife skills, how to season food properly, and cook on a stove. A great many American Protestant leaders of the past several decades have done something like this: Technological fads and church growth techniques occupy more of our attention than the Word of God. This has resulted in a diminished church which has not been properly formed in 'the culture of the Word.' If you are concerned about these things and seeking direction back toward those forgotten basics, this book will help to guide you back home."

—**JAKE MEADOR**, editor in chief of *Mere Orthodoxy*; author of *What Are Christians For?* and *In Search of the Common Good*

"God creates through his Word. His Word is about Jesus Christ, causing a society to erupt ithin the world—a culture wrapped around Christ himself emerging within the surrounding culture through the church's worship. God would have it no other way than his people being born from above by his power to speak spiritual realities into existence. This book will help you marvel again at God's power to work through his Word for all that we need."

—**HARRISON PERKINS,** pastor of Oakland Hills Community Church (OPC), Michigan; author of *Reformed Covenant Theology*

"Senkbeil and Woodford condense their post-Christian pocket-sized ecclesiology into one sentence: 'The word grows by itself—sometimes with spectacular results and sometimes not. But the word always brings the results God wills.' Absolutely so! As they unpack this truth, they free anxious pastors and committed lay people from the siren call of relevance (whether of the progressive or traditionalist variety) and focus them on their main, liberating task: exposing people to the Word so that the Word can do its work."

—**TIM PERRY,** lead pastor, St. Paul's Evangelical Lutheran Church, Steinbach, MB, Canada; author of *When Politics Becomes Heresy*

"This book cuts like a two-edged sword through the Church's capitulation to cultural trends in the name of mission. Senkbeil and Woodford call us back to a biblically grounded, Christ-centered witness that refuses to compromise. If you care about the Church's future in the West—and long to see it built on faithfulness rather than fads—this book is a must read."

—**BRYAN STECKER**, pastor, Trinity Lutheran, Waconia, Minnesota; founder of Lutheran Institute of Theology; host of *On The Line*

The Culture *of* God's Word

The Culture *of* God's Word

FAITHFUL MINISTRY IN A POST-CHRISTIAN SOCIETY

Harold L. Senkbeil
&
Lucas V. Woodford

LEXHAM PRESS

The Culture of God's Word: Faithful Ministry in a Post-Christian Society

Lexham Press, 1313 Bay St, Bellingham, WA 98225
LexhamPress.com

Print ISBN 9781683598930
Digital ISBN 9781683598947
Library of Congress Control Number 2025935883

Lexham Editorial: Todd Hains, Allisyn Ma, Jessi Strong, Danielle Burlaga, Mandi Newell
Cover Design: Sarah Brossow
Typesetting: Abigail Stocker

25 26 27 28 29 30 31 / IN / 12 11 10 9 8 7 6 5 4 3 2 1

Contents

Prayer for the Holy Spirit

Since the earliest days of the church, Christians have used Holy Scripture to shape and inform their prayers. The structured prayer below invites pastors and laity to pray for the Holy Spirit's blessing on the church as she proclaims Jesus Christ to the diverse peoples of the world and welcomes them into the culture of God's word.

It can be used by either individuals or groups—in which case a designated leader begins and others pray the words in bold print.

In the Name of the Father and of the Son
and of the Holy Spirit.
Amen.

O Lord, open my lips,
And my mouth will declare your praise. *Ps 51:15*

Forever, O Lord, your word
is firmly fixed in the heavens.

Your faithfulness endures to all generations;
you have established the earth, and it stands fast.

By your appointment they stand this day,
for all things are your servants.

I will never forget your precepts,
for by them you have given me life.

I am yours; save me,
for I have sought your precepts. *Ps 119:89–94*

I bow down toward your holy temple
**and give thanks to your name for your steadfast love
and your faithfulness,**
for you have exalted above all things
your name and your word. *Ps 138:2*

Let us pray.

O Almighty God, who at Pentecost sent down the Holy Spirit, the Comforter, to enlighten and empower your church to be a bright beacon of light and truth in Christ Jesus for all the world: Bestow upon us and all your faithful people his manifold gifts of grace, that we may believe your holy word and lead godly lives according to it, that many may see our good works and glorify you through faith in Jesus Christ our Lord.
Amen.

Lord, in your mercy,

Hear our prayer.

That your mighty word may take root and grow among us
for the joy and edification of Christ's holy people
and the salvation of many.
That we may cling to your word which alone brings life
as we bear joyful testimony to Jesus and his cross.
That you may sanctify us by your holy word
and thus keep us safe from the attacks of the Evil One.

Lord, in your mercy,

Hear our prayer.

That your faithful people may open their hearts and homes
to all nations of the earth and welcome strangers
to find refuge in the culture of the word.
That your holy church may be a home for the lost and weary
and an oasis of life and peace in a dark, despairing world.
That your word may bear abundant fruit in those who hear;
your will be done
and your kingdom come on earth
as it is already in heaven.

Lord, in your mercy,

Hear our prayer.

Our Father, who art in heaven,
hallowed be thy Name,
thy kingdom come,
thy will be done
on earth as it is in heaven.
Give us this day our daily bread.
And forgive us our trespasses,
as we forgive those who trespass against us.
And lead us not into temptation,
but deliver us from evil. *Matt 6:9–13*
For thine is the kingdom and the power, and the glory,
forever and ever. Amen.

Let us bless the Lord.

Thanks be to God.

The Lord bless us, protect us from all evil,
and bring us to everlasting life.

Amen.

PROLOGUE

Planting and Reaping the Word of God

Christians in the West stand at an uneasy crossroads. Christendom has ended. The church has lost her long-privileged place in society. Her boom years are over. The Christian morality that once guided the West is now but a vestige, seen as not only quaint and antiquated but inimical to human flourishing. The challenge is daunting.

Wave after wave of innovative approaches were introduced in the twentieth century to grow the church. Many of these outmoded evangelistic efforts were labeled as "contextualization"—the idea that if the church wants to effectively reach out, it must contextualize its message so people find it familiar and attractive. In this approach, human culture sets the agenda for the word.

Still the church continues to decline precipitously while the culture breeds an increasingly permissive society, not bound to any divinely established order. Contextualizing the gospel for successful evangelism in a secularized world of burgeoning paganism is a recipe for spiritual disaster. Shaping our missional efforts according to cultural trends only puts an expiration date on the church.

This book proposes an entirely different model—one rooted in the Bible itself. The book of Acts is a practical guide to mission in every generation. It shows how the first Christians were driven not by their cultural context but by the word of Christ to change the hearts and lives of people living very much in the world, yet not of it. They weren't seeking to convert cultures but people who lived in various cultures.

Faithful mission in a chaotic world builds on this New Testament template; people in every context—every nation, tribe, and language—should be acculturated by the word of Christ. For two millennia Christians have held that the church cultivates its own transcendent culture in a rapidly shifting social context—the culture of the word. The field is the world. The seed is the word. The word grows and cultivates its own unique culture. You could put it this way: as the word is sown, the culture is grown.

It's time to reclaim that approach for the present uncertain moment. Let's get planting! The seeding may be difficult, but harvesttime is coming. Those who sow in tears shall reap with shouts of joy (Ps 126:5).

Harold L. Senkbeil
Lucas V. Woodford
The Ascension of our Lord, 2024

CHAPTER 1

The Church Is Created by the Word of God

"For this reason the Jews seized me in the temple and tried to kill me. To this day I have had the help that comes from God, and so I stand here testifying both to small and great, saying nothing but what the prophets and Moses said would come to pass: that the Christ must suffer and that, by being the first to rise from the dead, he would proclaim light both to our people and to the Gentiles." And as he was saying these things in his defense, Festus said with a loud voice, "Paul, you are out of your mind; your great learning is driving you out of your mind."

Acts 26:21–24

Festus had a strong reaction to Paul presenting the gospel: "You're out of your mind!" But the apostle Paul wasn't the only person to get that response. Since the advent of Christianity, Christians have been more often than not standing on the outside of culture looking in. This can lead people to think they are just slightly odd or sometimes even outright dangerous. Both reactions can be found in the book of Acts.

After being apprehended by the temple authorities (Acts 21:27–36), Paul found himself in a political and cultural no-man's-land, a pawn in the legal chess game between the Roman procurator in Caesarea and the Jewish Sanhedrin in Jerusalem (Acts 23–24). Finally, after two years of imprisonment, Paul had his day in court before the new procurator (Porcius Festus), the Jewish client king (Herod Agrippa II), and Agrippa's sister (Bernice) (Acts 25). He laid out his exemplary life as an observant Jew, his initial virulent persecution of Christians, and his miraculous conversion on the Damascus road, and he presented an eloquent and persuasive argument for the gospel of Jesus's cross and resurrection. Procurator Festus accused him of lunacy, even though King Agrippa found Paul's defense persuasive (26:24–28).

Shifting Culture

The striking culture of the word creates tension in this fallen world. That tension increases as cultural drift accelerates.

Today, even gentle advocates of biblical standards sometimes get labeled as bigots or haters. It's tempting in our hostile social climate to become cultural warriors, trying to put the shattered pieces of Christendom back together again. Some people think if only we could discover how things came off the rails in the first place, maybe we could regain happier and more comfortable days for the people of God.

But it's a fool's errand. The tide of cultural disintegration rolls relentlessly on, sweeping up everything and everyone in its path. Besides, the myriad political, social, and philosophical influences that gave rise to this situation over the centuries defy accurate analysis and remedy.

Of course, missionaries and evangelists should study political history, ideological trends, and social psychology, but it's no use scrambling to get ahead of social trends that oppose the faith. There's a better path. The vitality and growth of Christ's church is not rooted in the shifting sands of cultural trends but the living and abiding word of God. The book of Acts provides a blueprint for confident mission in a shifting culture. The story of the growth of the church in that antagonistic setting is the story of the word of God in action. In fact, not once but three times in Acts we find explicit references to the growth of God's word (6:7; 12:24; 19:20).

The power for the growth of the kingdom is in the word itself. Jesus taught in the parable of the sower, "The seed is the word of God" (Luke 8:11). Despite the setting or context, concerted opposition or determined enemies, the power for the growth of the kingdom is never in those who proclaim and teach but in the word they proclaim and teach. The word grows by itself—sometimes with spectacular results and sometimes not. But the word always brings the results God wills (Isa 55:10–11).

Abiding Word

Human culture wields extraordinary influence on how people live and work, and of course that needs to be considered in evangelizing the actual world we live in. This is only common sense. Accurate communication of words—especially God's word—cannot take place apart from it. But addressing cultural context should be in service to the word, not the other way around. The word of God always takes priority over context. In fact, the word creates its own unique and transcendent culture that undergirds, shapes, and directs the mission and life of the holy Christian church on earth until Jesus comes again.

The book of Acts begins with the dramatic story of how the church was birthed in Jerusalem by the Spirit working through the word. The living and abiding word of God bridged sixteen diverse cultures when the apostles spoke the mighty works of God in their own tongues "as the Spirit gave them utterance" (Acts 2:4). All were amazed, though some doubted and mocked, contending the preachers were drunk (2:12). Peter stood up and proclaimed Jesus of Nazareth as both Lord and

Christ, put to death for their offenses and raised again for their justification. He invited all to repentance and baptism in the name of Jesus Christ for the forgiveness of their sins and the reception of the Holy Spirit (2:14–40). The seed of the word of God was growing and producing fruit; three thousand souls were baptized and added to the church that glorious Pentecost day (2:41).

But all was not well among the first believers. Soon internal dissension broke out among them over the distribution of support for widows. The twelve apostles gathered the believers together to get at the heart of the matter: "It is not right that we should give up preaching the word of God to serve tables. Therefore, brothers, pick out from among you seven men of good repute, full of the Spirit and of wisdom, whom we will appoint to this duty. But we will devote ourselves to prayer and to the ministry of the word" (Acts 6:2–4). Seven deacons were selected and publicly authorized to attend to secondary matters while the apostles focused on corporate worship (prayer) and preaching and pastoral care (the ministry of the word). They were intent on keeping central the main points in the life of Christ's church.

Luke documents the striking impact of God's word on the life and growth of the first Christian congregation: "And the word of God continued to increase, and the number of the disciples multiplied greatly in Jerusalem, and a great many of the priests became obedient to the faith" (Acts 6:7).

Concentrating on the numerical growth of the church to the exclusion of all else has proven less than fruitful in recent generations. The people before us are not potential recruits in a culture war we're fighting but lost souls seeking a hope which spans all generations, cultures, and time. In order for the world to see the word in action, we must live according to the word. Perhaps it's time to take a page from the first Christians and put the emphasis on the growth of the word of God among Christians—and through them to a watching world.

Our Dying World

The twentieth century was the bloodiest in human history. Wars and rumors of wars have plagued humankind since time immemorial, but modern mechanized killing on battlefields and organized oppression and genocide among nations resulted in mind-numbing numbers of casualties. Mass depravations and deportations, to say nothing of deliberate extermination in death camps, resulted in the slaughter of millions in the Ottoman Empire, Russia, Africa, China, Germany, Thailand, and elsewhere.

But present circumstances aren't much better. Terrorist regimes abound around the planet. Endemic disease, famine, and death threaten economic and social stability; fears run rampant. Long-festering racial and ethnic injustice and atrocities spill over into public rage, resulting in rioting and looting.

Tempers flare and passions erupt, fanning ancient animosities into open conflict all around the globe, including here at home. Technological achievements threaten human integrity and rational discussion. The specter of nuclear war, long dormant and unthinkable, rears its ghastly head once again.

More subtle but even more dangerous for human flourishing is the assault on human dignity and identity. Defining distinctives of the sexual binary in human physiology and anatomy take a back seat to inner feelings and personal desires. In many countries marriage is a legal option for same-sex couples, with polyamorous groups of three or more sometimes given marital rights.[1] The conjugal bond between a child's father and mother is seemingly irrelevant to its flourishing. Preborn children are denied personhood, making them all the easier to abort and discard. Parents increasingly find the care and nurture of their offspring subject to legally imposed sex and gender ideologies. What will be the cost of this unprecedented social experiment?

This world has become a rather inhumane place to live. A deep emotional and spiritual famine has descended upon it. In search of something better, our culture has set off on an uncharted journey with no lodestar to guide it. With no anchor in what is timelessly good and true and beautiful, many drift aimlessly with no common heritage or purpose. The Christian scholar and social observer Anthony Esolen points out that we live in the "suburbs of the city of man."[2] It is a subhuman existence driven by private urges and personal impulses. When unfettered passions take over, humans become more like beasts than people.

A fear of missing out on this life drives people to anxiously pursue their earthly passions. There they find only disillusionment, emptiness, alienation, and despair. Although people are dying to live, they find themselves literally dying instead. Such is humanity's common plight after Eden: in Adam all die (1 Cor 15:22).

In short, there's nothing new under the sun. Mission in the current cultural environment faces many of the same obstacles as during the apostolic era. Both cultures are fundamentally pagan at their core. Although we live in what Charles Taylor has called a "secular age," he points out it is certainly not irreligious.[3]

Secularism includes religious trappings like firmly held secular creeds, dogmas, and beliefs, but it's not just a rationalistic phenomenon. Ross Douthat notes that "a profound religious experience or awakening" plays a prominent role for many supposedly secular Americans.[4] What many call secularization is not actually a loss of religiosity but a return to ancient paganism—a seeking of divine power in the world (or the self) rather than outside of it with the gods themselves considered as part of nature. In our secularized neopagan world, meaning is found in things immanent rather than transcendent.[5]

Ultimately, the context for mission in the twenty-first century is the same as it's been throughout the history of the holy Christian church: Because of Adam's sin, we live perennially in a dying world. Despite its many joys and pleasures, life in God's good creation is not what he intended it to be in the beginning. The world we live in is marred by decay and death.

But just as in Adam all shall die, so shall all in the Lord Jesus Christ be made alive (1 Cor 15:22). The word of God took root and grew in the pagan world of the first century, and it can and will make a difference in our own pagan time. The culture of the word always brings the life that is in Christ Jesus to this dying world (2 Cor 4:11).

Colliding Cultures

How can we bridge the widening culture gap between the church and a secularized world? In our ever-changing society, rapidly shifting values make it next to impossible to be "all things to all people" (1 Cor 9:22).

Yet even amid a cacophony of cultures, the compelling culture of the word meets the same deeply felt human needs as it did in antiquity. No matter which languages, skin colors, or other diversities exist in our neighborhoods, everybody shares the same twofold spiritual dilemma. They're simultaneously sinners and sinned against—perpetrators as well as victims of sin. Sin's ultimate consequence confronts us all: death in all its dimensions (bodily, spiritually, and emotionally). This is square one in missional outreach in an increasingly complex and diverse world. The ultimate human problem is death—in all its facets.

Into this dying world, the word of God brings life eternal. Wherever his word is proclaimed and embraced by faith, it creates its own unique culture, bestowing life in all its fullness through faith in Jesus Christ (John 10:10). Wherever the word is sown and takes root, it grows its own culture.

The Great Invasion

In the beginning when the world was young, God spoke, and he has never stopped. He kept right on speaking to every subsequent generation, but then he did something truly extraordinary. God, who is pure spirit, took on flesh so that he could speak to us more intimately and directly as an embodied Word (Heb 1:1–2).

When Quirinius was governor in Syria and Caesar Augustus ruled in far-off Rome (Luke 2:1–2), the Son of God came down from heaven and took up residence in the womb of a young virgin girl in Nazareth (Matt 1:18–25). When the fullness of time had come, God sent forth his Son (Gal 4:4). Like Father, like Son; Jesus came speaking the words given him by his Father in heaven and doing his Father's will. He was intent on the Father's mission to seek and save a lost humanity, so he did what the Father gave him to do and he said the words the Father gave him to say.

> And Jesus cried out and said, "Whoever believes in me, believes not in me but in him who sent me. And whoever sees me sees him who sent me. I have come into the world as light, so that whoever believes in me may not remain in darkness. If anyone hears my words and does not keep them, I do not judge him; for I did not come to judge the world but to save the world. The one who rejects me and does not receive my words has a judge; the word that I have spoken will judge him on the last day. For I have not spoken on my own authority, but the Father who sent me has himself given me a commandment—what to say and what to speak. And I know that his commandment is eternal life. What I say, therefore, I say as the Father has told me." (John 12:44–50)

In every generation, Christian life and mission revolves around the person of Jesus and his life-giving word. Like the first Christians in Jerusalem, we can have confidence in his word. The word of God continues to grow and increase according to God's own will and purpose—in good times and bad.

The Word Faces Opposition

There was an initial time of comparative tranquility for the apostolic church after the conversion of Saul when he began proclaiming Jesus in the synagogues and was approved by the disciples in Jerusalem as one of them. The church began to grow and prosper: "So the church throughout all Judea and Galilee and Samaria had peace and was being built up" (Acts 9:31). Antioch became a hub of vibrant Christian outreach, where Barnabus and Saul diligently instructed the faithful: "In Antioch the disciples were first called Christians" (11:26). Antioch became the vibrant base of active mission in word and deed. Things were looking up.

But then the tide changed: "About that time Herod the king laid violent hands on some who belonged to the church" (Acts 12:1). First, he executed James, then he seized Peter, locking him in prison. The very night Herod wanted to follow up with Peter, he was miraculously delivered from his prison cell (12:6–17).

Having been stymied in his efforts to stamp out Christian preaching, King Herod abandoned Jerusalem for the refuge of his headquarters in Caesarea. There he ultimately breathed his last, struck down by an angel of the Lord because of his blasphemy (12:23). Despite the deliberate opposition of Herod's machinations, Luke explains: "But the word of God increased and multiplied" (12:24). Jesus's life-giving word could not be struck down by human means.

The Embodied Word

The foundation for Christian life and mission stays the same in every era: Jesus Christ, the eternal Word of the Father, embodied in living human flesh. John unfolds this central mystery of the Christian faith in the elegant prologue to his gospel: "In the beginning was the Word, and the Word was with God, and the Word was God" (John 1:1). This one sentence links the Old Testament with the New.

What God started at the beginning of creation he continues in Jesus. By the sheer power of God's word, all creation sprang into existence. His word was there from the start. In fact, so closely linked was God with his creative word, that this word actually was God the Son, existing eternally and present from the dawn of creation. But then millennia later, in the fullness of time, God sent forth his Son to be born in human flesh (Gal 4:4). In Jesus, the creative word who is God from all eternity took on human flesh to dwell on planet earth (John 1:14).

John the beloved disciple was among those privileged to walk and talk with Jesus, to touch him and listen to him, and to visually witness all that he said and did. "We have seen his glory," John wrote, "glory as of the only Son of the Father, full of grace and truth" (John 1:14). What he heard and saw and touched concerning this embodied Word of life he proclaimed through his apostolic letter (1 John 1:1–3).

The Written Word

But John lived a long time ago and very far away. How can we today access what he heard, saw, and handled concerning Jesus, the embodied Word of the Father? We have that Word in writing. "We were with him on the holy mountain," Peter wrote

(2 Pet 1:18). The apostles wrote down what Jesus did and said, guided by the Holy Spirit. The Bible is not some collection of obscure ancient texts to be deconstructed and tweaked to fit current cultural trends and ideologies. Paul pointed Timothy to the Bible as a sure and certain foundation of truth and life in Jesus: "All Scripture is breathed out by God and profitable for teaching, for reproof, for correction, and for training in righteousness" (2 Tim 3:16).

The Inspired Word

The heart and center of the life of Christ's church in the New Testament is the person and work of the Holy Spirit. That remains true for us today. The written word of God is the sword of the Spirit (Eph 6:17) and the sole source and norm of all Christian teaching. It is "breathed out by God" (2 Tim 3:16). The Bible is God's inspired word—God-breathed by God's own Spirit. The word of God gives the Spirit of God. Scripture is not merely truthful and accurate in all that it says but filled with the power and presence of the Holy Spirit to bring people to faith and keep them in the faith once delivered to the saints (Jude 1:3). Peter witnessed this firsthand as he evangelized Cornelius and his extended gentile household: "While Peter was still saying these things, the Holy Spirit fell on all who heard the word" (Acts 10:44).

The Bible is not just a collection of human words about God, but God's word in human language, as Peter himself declared: "For no prophecy was ever produced by the will of man, but men spoke from God as they were carried along by the Holy Spirit" (2 Pet 1:21). Although reason, experience, and tradition have a role in the life and mission of the church, they must be subordinate to the word. God's word always takes priority.

The Bible is the written word of the living Word of God the Father. This word calls us to share it, to be people of mission. People in every cultural context—especially one as deeply inhumane as ours—need that word in order to live. The church must uphold the word in all its truth and splendor, proclaiming law and gospel to one and all. Our contemporaries are starving to death spiritually. The devil, world, and sinful flesh relentlessly threaten them with death and destruction. They desperately need the nutrients God provides in his holy word.

The Nourishing Word

Jesus famously fended off the devil's first temptation in the wilderness with the bold assertion that the word of God provides essential nourishment by quoting from the Old Testament: "Man does not live by bread alone, but man lives by every word that comes from the mouth of the LORD" (Deut 8:3).

Christ Jesus came down from heaven to bring life into the world. As the embodied Word of the living Father, he is not only alive himself but gives life to all who believe in him in this dying world. Everything Jesus did and taught pulses with divine life. "I am the living bread that came down from heaven," he told his disciples. "If anyone eats of this bread, he will live forever. And the bread that I will give for the life of the world is my flesh" (John 6:51).[6]

The Bible is not some spiritual charm or just another ancient text that needs reshaping to fit the moral and cultural climate of our time. The word of God is still alive and active. It throbs with the vitality of Jesus himself, who is the Word of God embodied in human flesh. His words bring his divine life to our dying world in every age throughout history, including our own.

The Performative Word

Many view the primary life and work of the church in terms of education and promotion. Emotional worship events are designed to tug at the heart, while sermons assure people that God loves them and outline foundational biblical principles for Christian living. Has the church wittingly or unwittingly moved away from a culture of the word? Have we moved away from the apostles' teaching and the fellowship, the breaking of bread, and prayers to something simply reflecting general secular culture?

To be sure, quality teaching remains critical, but faithful preaching is the heart of the matter. People need Jesus. And Jesus is present in his word (Matt 18:20). The word brings all of Jesus with all the gifts he earned by his life, death, and resurrection: forgiveness, life, and salvation for penitent sinners. God's word speaks realities, not mere spiritual or emotional concepts. Worship, therefore, is far more than just an emotional high. It's the experience of the life-giving presence of the living God among his people by the word proclaimed and the sacraments administered in Jesus's name and stead. The word of God always does what it says; it frees people from spiritual bondage and enlivens them with the life that is in Christ Jesus. Can we trust it to do what it promises?

Emancipation for Sinners

The fundamental problem of unbelievers isn't mere spiritual ignorance. Rather, they—like all of us—are sin addicts. Not only do they commit sin, but like all addicts, they think that the only way out is to indulge their cravings even more. Moreover, they're not only sinners; they are sinned against and constantly struggle with the wounds and fallout of other people's sins in terms of continuing shame and emotional distress. It's not a case of ignorance but spiritual bondage. This can be seen in Jesus's conversation with the believing Jews:

> So Jesus said to the Jews who had believed him, "If you abide in my word, you are truly my disciples, and you will know the truth, and the truth will set you free."
>
> They answered him, "We are offspring of Abraham and have never been enslaved to anyone. How is it that you say, 'You will become free'?"

> Jesus answered them, "Truly, truly, I say to you, everyone who practices sin is a slave to sin. The slave does not remain in the house forever; the son remains forever. So if the Son sets you free, you will be free indeed." (John 8:31–36)

Mission in our troubled era involves far more than simple obedience to the so-called Great Commission[7] or the laudable desire to bring salvation to sinners. After all, many today dispute the very category of sin—much less eternal punishment. They may be able to identify wrongs people have done to them, but they're at a loss to recognize sins they've committed against God. So, we need an adept mission paradigm in a world that has lost its compass spiritually speaking.

Like Jesus himself, we need to see suffering people as sheep without a shepherd—lost and helpless (Matt 9:36). Like all addicts, they need rescue and recovery. Dying and in bondage to sin and death, they're in desperate need of the life embodied in Jesus and his life-giving word.

The implications are clear. From generation to generation, down through the centuries, in each and every era, the word of God continues to grow and to bring the life that is in Jesus. To receive life in a dying world, people need to enter into a new and transcendent culture—the culture God himself grows in his church by means of his life-giving, death-destroying word.[8]

Imagination in Mission

Of course there is still a need for creativity in mission. Innovation and adaptability are good things in service of the gospel. As pastors in different generations, we have each been creative and energetic in mission in our own way. Harold served as a missionary and church planter decades ago; Lucas earned a doctorate in evangelism and outreach and now serves as a bishop, supporting the growth of Christ's kingdom creatively and pastorally in the face of growing social turmoil and cultural antagonism.

Yet while creativity and innovation have their place, all too often human ingenuity leads to something other than a culture of the word. While novelty may be well-intentioned, it too often robs Christ's mission of the vitality he seeks to provide by his clear word. That word remains powerful enough to overcome opposition of all sorts, including the downtrend of the Western church.

The decline of the church in the West has caused a lot of hand-wringing. It manifests in two extreme reactions: anxiety and panic or immobilization and inaction. Trusting the power of the word gives us wisdom to act strategically and urgently given the facts and avoid unnecessary anxiety and panic, which leads to bad decisions. Like walking on a log over a river, we must keep our balance or we will fall off either into panic or inaction. These attitudes betray a distrust in God's word, which declares the gates of hell will not prevail against

Christ's church (Matt 16:18), and it instructs the church and her pastors to "preach the word" and to "be ready in season and out of season" (2 Tim 4:2).

Faith requires we act with urgency and decisiveness in the face of adversity. Like the word itself, faith is busy and active. It's always in motion, clinging to Christ and loving others. A culture of the word instills in us the confidence to maintain a nonanxious presence as we navigate the challenges of our day. To develop the culture of the word in the church requires that the word be regularly sown in her midst. That's why our mantra is as the word is sown, the culture is grown.

Mission and Opposition

The apostolic church faced an antagonistic culture much more like ours than the comparatively friendly culture during the era of Christendom. The book of Acts records many spectacular conversion stories and the rapid spreading of the word but also episodes of persecution and near disaster. Yet the golden thread of the power and presence of Jesus runs through them all by the preaching and teaching of his word. The word always has its way, no matter its enemies—be they human or demonic.

In Ephesus, Paul had a skirmish with the powers of darkness when itinerant Jewish exorcists tried to use the name of "the Jesus whom Paul proclaims" as a magic spell to cast out demons (Acts 19:13). The possessed man reacted violently to their misuse of God's power, and he chased them away, leaving them naked and wounded. Upon seeing the power of the word of the Lord, many citizens of Ephesus came to believe in Jesus and turned from their practices of witchcraft and the occult. They publicly burned their books of magic. Yet despite Paul's victory over Satan's power, credit is given not to him but to the word he preached: "So *the word of the Lord continued to increase* and prevail mightily" (Acts 19:20, emphasis added).

Hearers and Doers

How do we stay true to a culture of the word and move forward in mission? Re-envisioning our purpose is the first and essential step in recovering vitality for outreach in times of opposition. The people of God need to see things his way despite prevailing cultural winds to the contrary. Pastors and missionaries need to be good eye doctors, as Kevin Vanhoozer puts it:

> The church, the body of Christ, has a vision problem. This could be diagnosed as a culturally induced myopia that allows us to see only what is in the material world immediately in front of us. Or perhaps the problem is an astigmatism that prevents the light of what can be known of God in creation from shining through. In either case, the pastor-theologian can help by giving congregations the corrective lenses of Scripture, which Calvin calls the "spectacles" that allow us to read the world rightly.[9]

Along with correcting our vision to align with God's, our hearing needs to be checked. Jesus stressed the connection between hearing his word and doing it. When his friends told him his mother and brothers could not reach him because of the press of the crowd, he replied, "My mother and brothers are those who hear the word of God and do it" (Luke 8:21). As the heart of mission, the text of holy Scripture is never inert. It's forever a performative word; it always does what it says. A focus on God's word does not foster apathy or business as usual in the church. Instead, it enlivens and activates vigorous mission.

That's the thing about the word of God; it is a living, busy, active thing. It's busy creating the very realities it speaks about. The apostle James has a challenge for us all: "Be doers of the word, and not hearers only, deceiving yourselves. ... The one who looks into the perfect law, the law of liberty, and perseveres, being no hearer who forgets but a doer who acts, he will be blessed in his doing" (Jas 1:22, 25).

That living, busy, active word gathers people from every context into God's transcendent culture to bring them life for time and eternity. As the word is sown, the culture is grown.

CHAPTER 2

The Church Lives in One Transcendent Culture

And they stirred up the people and the elders and the scribes, and they came upon [Stephen] and seized him and brought him before the council, and they set up false witnesses who said, "This man never ceases to speak words against this holy place and the law, for we have heard him say that this Jesus of Nazareth will destroy this place and will change the customs that Moses delivered to us."

Acts 6:12–14

The Jews of the New Testament era prized their identity as heirs of Abraham, Isaac, and Jacob; they were God's chosen people in whom all the nations of the earth would be blessed (Gen 22:18). They were especially wary of people like Stephen—outsiders whom they saw as a threat against the Torah and the sacrifices of the Lord's house, the sacred temple where God condescended to dwell among them.

The church is the New Testament Israel, built on the foundation of the apostles and prophets (Eph 2:20). Like the Jews, Christians understood they were called out of the world to live in a distinct, yet transcendent, culture. The word of God gathers people into one earthly and heavenly assembly called the church or the *ekklesia* (the "called out ones").

But what do we mean when we say "church"? A merely institutional view of the church is wrong. Although congregations may adopt organizational constitutions and corresponding bureaucratic structures, the church properly speaking is not a human organization but a divine organism—the living body of Christ (Col 1:24). When the focus remains on the physical institution of the church, congregations seek "converts" to keep their struggling bureaucratic structures alive financially. This tendency toward institutionalism hinders agile and proactive mission—be that among leaders of church bodies or in local congregations. Fighting to preserve a purely human institution at all costs blinds the church to its actual mission. This is not the church as she really is.

When Jesus speaks of "my church," he means all people in any era who, by the power of the Holy Spirit, have been brought to faith in him as both Lord and God. These souls are quite literally called out of the world into an assembly that is simultaneously one, holy, and catholic (universal). Acts illustrates how the church's catholicity encompasses diverse human cultures. It includes the first multiethnic converts at Pentecost, the Ethiopian eunuch whom Philip evangelized, and the multitude of converts Paul pastored throughout his three Mediterranean missionary journeys. And that was just the beginning. From first-century prophets and apostles, to the great Reformers of the Middle Ages, to dedicated missionaries and martyrs in more recent eras, a great cloud of witnesses surrounds us still today (Heb 12:1). Two millennia of history has demonstrated the vastness of Christ's church.

Thus, the church is far bigger than any local assembly or outward association of like-minded congregations. Peter, and then later the whole church in Jerusalem, learned that the Lord had opened the church to include the gentiles. Paul would eventually shake the dust from his clothes as a protest against Jewish recalcitrancy and go exclusively to the gentiles (Acts 18:6). It would take years of struggle for many Jewish converts to look beyond a narrowly institutional view of God's kingdom.

Yet, many Christians still struggle with institutionalism. The late Christian apologist C. S. Lewis mocked the narrowminded parochial view held by many regarding the church. In Lewis's fanciful collection of letters between demons, the experienced tempter, Screwtape, consoles his novice nephew Wormwood, who is despairing because his "patient" has joined a church.

> One of our great allies at present is the Church itself. Do not misunderstand me. I do not mean the Church as we see her spread out through all time and space and rooted in eternity, terrible as an army with banners. That, I confess, is a spectacle which makes our boldest tempters uneasy. But fortunately it is quite invisible to those humans.[10]

This eternally holy Christian church—this communion of saints—transcends the boundaries of time and eternity. It incorporates men, women, and children of every nation, from all tribes and peoples and languages (Rev 7:9). This is the church as she really is. Not our church, not your church, not someone else's church, but *the* church.

Paul stressed this all-encompassing understanding of the church in his final words to the elders of the congregation in Ephesus. He instructed them, "Pay careful attention to yourselves and all the flock, in which the Holy Spirit has made you overseers, to care for the church of God, which he obtained with his own blood" (Acts 20:28). Later he exhorted them to remember the source of the church's true unity: "There is one body, and one Spirit—just as you were called to the one hope that belongs to your call—one Lord, one faith, one baptism, one God and Father of all, who is over all and through all and in all" (Eph 4:4–5).

Dogma remains essential. The Lord builds his church on but one faith founded in holy Scripture: "There is neither Jew nor Greek, there is neither slave nor free, there is no male and female, for you are all one in Christ Jesus" (Gal 3:28).

The true nature of the church extends beyond the limitations of human institutional trappings. With all her warts and blemishes, the church remains Christ's bride for whom he laid down his life to cleanse her with his blood to be his very own for time and eternity. But how will the church teach this comprehensive unity of the culture of the word across the vast chasms of human cultural diversity?

Contextualization

Effective communication of the gospel in any locale uses the artifacts, language, and signs specific to that particular human culture. Commonsense contextualization is needed and relies on using basic communication skills. Acts illustrates this well. When Peter preached to Jews on the day of Pentecost in the very shadow of the temple in Jerusalem, his sermon was laced with quotations from the Old Testament prophets they knew well (Acts 2:14–36).

But soon Peter found himself preaching to an entirely different audience. Before long the Holy Spirit led him to Caesarea, the seat of Rome's government, and to the home of Cornelius, a Roman officer. There Peter proclaimed Jesus and the forgiveness of sins in his name to Cornelius's friends and relatives (Acts 10:34–43): "He is Lord of all" (10:36). Jesus came not just to rescue and save God's people Israel but through them to reach into every land and custom and language with the saving message of his cross and resurrection. Peter's Caesarea sermon had the same content as his sermon in Jerusalem, but it was for different people and therefore tailored to their particular experience and needs.

It's the same today. If you're talking to rural folks, you use different terminology than among corporate executives. Community outreach in the great urban centers of our nation incorporates the diverse customs and dialects of various subcultures and ethnicities. Cultural context is crucial when communicating the gospel, but context never overshadows the text of holy Scripture.

Shifting Mission Situations

Acts records a whole series of mini Pentecosts as the Holy Spirit called, gathered, and enlightened people, including all kinds of people that first congregation in Jerusalem could have never anticipated. Imagine how the first disciples must have felt as they looked back on the familiar Galilean culture they had left, the one they knew so well, felt at home in, and likely treasured in their hearts. They were uprooted from everything comfortable and familiar as they experienced new peoples, languages, sights, smells, and tastes. But to all those strangers in diverse foreign contexts and customs, they spoke one and the same living message of the resurrected Christ.

The North American cultural context has dramatically shifted as well. The church finds herself in a diminished social position compared to past eras. Christendom—the alliance between church, state, and society—began with the Edict of Milan (AD 313), when the Roman emperor Constantine officially ended religious persecution. Over time, the church gained great political and social privilege as Christianity gradually became the official state religion. Church buildings were erected across the empire using government funds, and Christian dogma began to influence morality and public policy. Before long, a clerical hierarchy developed and flourished, and the church assumed a larger and larger role in civilized society throughout the Mediterranean world. In time, the line between sacred and secular was blurred and then finally erased. The Constantinian alliance between state and church eventually became a de facto merger as Christian bishops assumed civil authority. By the early medieval period, an emperor was crowned by the Pope.[11]

The Rise of Christendom

This Constantinian arrangement cast its shadow well into the Renaissance and beyond. The Protestant Reformation had as many political and cultural features as ecclesial implications. It brought not only doctrinal conflict and church divisions but political struggles and intrigue as well. The resulting bloodshed and warfare eventually engulfed most of central Europe. An uneasy compromise enacted in the Peace of Augsburg (1555) enshrined the principle of *cuius regio, eius religio* ("whose the rule, his the religion"). Churches under the jurisdiction of a Protestant sovereign became Protestant, while those under Catholic princes remained Catholic. Gradually this arrangement was set aside and a multiplicity of Christian denominations and sects arose, especially in America after European settlers brought their multiple faith traditions to these new shores.

For almost a millennium in the West, the link between faith and life dominated and stayed inviolable. Christendom became the defining feature of Western culture. Daily life and commerce transpired under a pervasive Christian veneer. Churches—of various confessions depending on the region—enjoyed both privilege and influence over public morality and thinking. Social pressure enforced Christian virtue, and biblical standards were the widely accepted norm. For centuries, culture did much of the heavy lifting when it came to teaching Christian virtue, even in churches. Though both of us were raised in two different generations in rural and small-town America (one in the '50s and the other in the '80s), we both assumed nearly all our neighbors were practicing Christians of one stripe or another.

But all that's gone now. Christendom has ended. The bond between church and society has been severed. Now Christianity is no longer the predominant force shaping public mores and influencing behavior. Segments of the broader American culture grow ever more hostile not just toward Christian teachings but Christian churches in general—even some Christians personally. In such a world, it's easy to look wistfully at the past through rose-colored glasses.

The Pentecost Impact

Even the disciples got caught up in nostalgia for the days of yore. After all the time and effort Jesus invested in teaching his disciples that his kingdom was radically unique and transcendent, they still longed for the return of the Davidic kingdom and its glory days long past. On the verge of Christ's ascension, they asked, "Lord, will you at this time restore the kingdom to Israel?" (Acts 1:6).

The Holy Spirit changed all that. Pentecost intervened, and people from every land and language heard the word of God in their own tongue. Jewish disciples observed outsiders from Samaria and Ethiopia coming to faith. Before long—especially through the work of Paul, the apostle to the gentiles—God's word was rapidly expanding across cultural barriers everywhere throughout the Mediterranean basin: "The word of the Lord continued to increase and prevail mightily" (Acts 19:20). The same men who once longed for the return of the fabled kingdom of David now began to see that by his word Jesus had inaugurated God's transcendent kingdom, embracing every tribe, people, and language.

We need to reexamine the world before us, just as they were forced to. We need to quit looking at the kingdom nostalgically through cultural rearview mirrors and see the possibilities before us in this new context as the culture of the word does its work.

Culture Wars

People have been talking about "culture wars" for several generations. As the gap widens between acceptable lifestyles in the church and in the world, tensions build. As a result, some see the primary Christian mission in this generation as changing the culture and returning to that happy era when churches were in a privileged position in society and Christian moral standards were widely held. Like those disciples captivated by the allure of the Davidic kingdom, they want to revive Christendom, turn the clock back, and restore the more comfortable norms of yesteryear.

We beg to differ. With roots in two different generations, both of us are keenly aware that the "good old days" were not all that good. Perhaps church attendance was more widely practiced and there were less social pressures against biblical morality decades ago, but familiarity can breed contempt. When Christianity was the expected social norm, hypocrisy ran rampant. We certainly don't need nostalgic culture warriors masquerading as Christian evangelists today, fighting to bring back Christendom while conveniently forgetting the maladies of those times. Shallow faith and cultural capitulation are a perennial temptation for Christians, and it's naïve to think previous generations knew how to effectively link belief and life uniformly to prevent immorality or unbelief.

To be sure, Christians are always called to be lights of civic duty and virtue for the good of humanity in their contemporary cultural setting. Yet Jesus never commissioned his church to evangelize cultures, but to evangelize people who live within cultures. Cultural sensitivity is an important ingredient in commonsense contextualization, but it's not the heart of mission. The biblical text remains primary when it comes to culturally sensitive evangelization and outreach.

What Is Culture?

What do we mean by culture? Jesus and the first Christians were Jews. They had a uniquely Jewish culture, reflected in the language they spoke, the clothes they wore, and the food they ate. Culture is simply the social environment people live in. If people were fish, it would be the water they swim in. Culture includes the speech idioms, attire, accepted social norms, and symbols of life that shape how people communicate and interact with others in a given time and place.

In his classic text exploring how Christians have historically related to human cultures, H. Richard Niebuhr says culture includes "language, habits, ideas, beliefs, customs, social organization, inherited artifacts, technical processes, and values."[12] He identifies five distinct ways Christians over the centuries have sought to live faithfully while relating to the culture around them: (1) Christ against culture, (2) the Christ of culture, (3) Christ above culture, (4) Christ and culture in paradox, and (5) Christ the transformer of culture. Niebuhr's categories attempt to codify how churches respond to radically shifting human cultures. Informed readers can draw their own conclusions of where our model fits in this taxonomy; elements of the latter three likely surface.

Christian evangelists, preachers, catechists, and curates today need to be at least as culturally sensitive as the disciples were in their first congregation in Jerusalem. The disciples learned a lesson in commonsense cultural contextualization when a rift between Hellenist and Hebrew Christians caused them to bring in seven deacons to attend to support services while they focused on public corporate prayers and the ministry of the word (Acts 6:3–4). They had to exercise holy discernment in addressing that issue, even as they carefully adapted to the needs at hand.

No matter which culture we're in, other cultures must be taken into consideration. Commonsense contextualization remains critical for effective communication, and it must be done with careful discernment. Cultural gaps are not insurmountable; overcoming diversity happens all through the book of Acts. The New Testament church demonstrated remarkable adaptive capacity. Amazing commonalities between divergent cultures are there if we just have eyes to see them. After all, we're diverse human beings made in the image and likeness of one and the same God.

Permanence and Change

The church's intersection with foreign cultures in the book of Acts lights the way for caring conversations in the name of Jesus in our own time. Amid rapidly shifting cultural contexts Christians need to learn and relearn how best to communicate what remains forever unchanging, God's word: "Forever, O LORD, your word is firmly set in the heavens" (Ps 119:89). The earliest Christians did it time and again, as evidenced by Peter's interaction with Cornelius the Roman centurion (Acts 10) as well as Philip's conversation with the Ethiopian court official (Acts 8). Later in Acts we see Paul navigating all sorts of language and cultural divisions throughout his missionary journeys, interacting comfortably with all kinds of people ranging from common laborers to kings and governors. The cultural context was changing, so he adjusted his approach accordingly.

Commonsense contextualizing exercised with holy discernment develops a salutary adaptive capacity. While important, these skills are not the mission of the church but a tool to allow the word to be sown so that the culture can be grown.

There's no denying change. The comparatively friendly cultural climate of the past has shifted radically. It's no use pretending otherwise. There's no going back to a more comfortable context. The world is in permanent flux, so the church needs to adjust its approach continually to meet people where they are at.

Yet it's foolish to chase after fads. If you try and keep up with the latest trend, you'll be in a constant scramble. If you try and ride ever-shifting cultural waves, you'll lose your balance; they crest and then fall again before you know it. When it comes to human culture, the present is always morphing into the past, giving way to yet another craze. Trendiness is appealing, but it doesn't work for the long haul. The next new thing approaches fast, only to vanish to make way for the next wave. Instead of playing catch up with cultural trends, it's better to root the church's mission in things lasting and solid: the abiding word of the Lord.

The word of the Lord stands forever, and the gospel message of Christ the crucified is true and unchanging. Commonsense dictates that one and the same gospel message needs to be communicated regardless of the time or culture we live in. People from all over the Mediterranean world—Pontus and

Asia, Egypt, Pamphylia and elsewhere—gathered in Jerusalem on Pentecost day. All heard one and the same message, "the mighty works of God," that bridged the many significant cultural gaps dividing them (Acts 2:11).

Text vs. Context

What the first Christians did in their time we can do now. In a chaotic social context, faithfulness and effectiveness seem always in tension. Text and context appear perpetually at odds when it comes to mission. The pertinent question is this: Which will it be? Does the biblical text or the cultural context determine the mission? Of course, both are in play. We must use the various artifacts and customs specific to any given cultural context to gain a hearing for the gospel. This is only common sense. The apostle Paul asserts his famous "all things to all people" approach to contextualization in his letter to the Corinthians:

> For though I am free from all, I have made myself a servant to all, that I might win more of them. To the Jews I became as a Jew, in order to win Jews. To those under the law I became as one under the law (though not being myself under the law) that I might win those under the law. To those outside the law I became as one outside the law (not being outside the law of God but under the law of Christ) that I might win those outside the law. To the weak I became weak, that I might win

> the weak. I have become all things to all people, that by all means I might save some. I do it all for the sake of the gospel, that I may share with them in its blessings. (1 Cor 9:19–23)

Paul's maxim of "all things to all people" is often misunderstood and misapplied, however. To reduce what he's saying to one single rigid tactic is to ignore the essential step of perceptive and compassionate soul care. Ultimately, it denies the power of the gospel that God uses to convert unbelieving hearts (Rom 1:16). It makes evangelism simply about methodology and contextualization strategies. We must never aim to evangelize people into some passing sociological human subculture but into the timeless transcendent company of all the faithful.

For Paul, becoming all things to all people does not sacrifice the church's transcendent unity for the sake of mission. While he was clearly focused on the commonsense context of personal relationships and mindsets, he proclaimed just the one transcendent gospel of Jesus and his cross for one and all (1 Cor 2:2). It's an impossibility to be all things to all people in a literal sense. Were he to choose one side or another in the American civil rights demonstrations in the '60s or in the racial riots of 2020, he would have alienated the opposition. He didn't aim to become exactly like each subculture to gain a hearing, such as changing his skin color, sleeping around to understand a prostitute's plight, or engaging in pagan worship to make pagans feel at home in the church. When Paul stressed being all things to all people, he meant he wanted to get inside their heads and hearts. He desired to compassionately understand what it's like to walk in their shoes and live in their circumstances even as he called them to a new and transformative life in Christ.

The culture of the word encompasses this kind of compassionate understanding, while acculturating individuals from distinctively different identities and customs into one overarching transcendent culture of the church universal and eternal. Paul's compassionate and considerate approach to gospel proclamation shows how to best foster the culture of the word. But there's no need to compromise Christian ethos or teaching to gain a hearing within a given subculture and grow the culture of the word.

What Is the Culture of the Word?

What do we mean by "culture of the word"? The culture of the word is the fullness of life enacted by the living and creative word of the triune God. His divinely generated culture embraces people of every language, race, and custom, and incorporates them into his transcendent and eternal kingdom. This approach brings simplicity and clarity to missiological chaos and confusion in every age. As the word is sown, the culture is grown.

The earliest evangelists weren't at all concerned that the world's script conflicted with the biblical script. Their confidence and hope were grounded in Christ Jesus and his unchanging word. Paul did not accommodate the text of God's word to the cultural mores of the time. He was not shy about labeling culturally sanctioned sexual and social aberrations as unacceptable and sinful. He was quick to point out, however, that people who had been rescued from that lifestyle by faith in Christ Jesus should be warmly welcomed into full Christian fellowship: "But you were washed, you were sanctified, you were justified in the name of the Lord Jesus Christ and by the Spirit of our God" (1 Cor 6:11).

We can learn from these earliest Christians. Instead of putting cultural context in the driver's seat for mission, the text of holy Scripture should steer the way. The most pressing need for the church's missionary task in this difficult cultural moment is not contextualization but textualization. Instead of crafting a separate message for every social and ethnic subculture, individuals from every language, people, and tribe should be incorporated into the church's own uniquely transcendent and eternal culture. In short, our aim is not to adapt the message to the culture but to acculturate people to the word of God.

Acculturation is different from enculturation. Enculturation happens naturally as people become accustomed to the culture they were born into. Acculturation involves the conscious effort to introduce people to an unfamiliar culture, so much so they become at home in it. Our mission in today's culture is to acculturate people into the transcendent culture of God's transforming word. We are not evangelizing a collapsing culture; we are evangelizing people who live within that culture to give them a hope and a future in Christ.

Consider what happened after Pentecost. The same gospel initially preached in Jerusalem was first taken to Judea, then Samaria, and finally the farthest ends of the earth (Acts 1:8). As the gospel spread in those radically different cultural contexts, the culture of the word transformed people from the many distinctive cultures of their homelands into citizens of one transcultural kingdom of God.

Missiological Mash-up

Today when the church seems everywhere in decline, we need to recover the church's historic stance toward her ever-shifting cultural setting. Paul boldly professed, "For I am not ashamed of the gospel, for it is the power of God for salvation to everyone who believes, to the Jew first and also to the Greek" (Rom 1:16). He saw no need to dress the gospel in trendy cultural fads or package Jesus in hot new attractive styles. Neither should we. Despite its practicality, human pragmatism has never been a defining mark of the church.

In the words of an old maxim, whoever marries the culture becomes an early widower. Yet current mission practices seem to ignore this principle. For more than a half century, every few years have introduced a new missiology, each promising to be the ultimate key to vibrant growth and vitality. The resulting mash-up has only compounded the confusion.

Those who follow church trends have seen the unabashed tongue-lashing the emergent church movement gave to the old church growth movement for its utter failure to deliver. But then just one short decade later, things shifted and the emergent church movement faded. Next came a refined missional movement, lifting up the central importance of contextualization and leaving behind the emergent movement.[13] Then came the urban church-planting movement promoting the latest approach: metrospirituality.[14] Multiple "laws" guaranteeing dramatic growth and vitality for a church in decline continue to proliferate, betraying a lack of confidence in the word and the culture it naturally grows.[15]

Though there's something to learn from each movement, they all deserve scrutiny. Every movement and subsequent development should be evaluated scripturally. "Test everything; hold fast what is good," Paul wrote to the church in Thessalonica (1 Thess 5:21). "Test the spirits to see whether they are from God" was John's directive (1 John 4:1). Peter, Paul, and Barnabas reported back to the church at Jerusalem on how their mission work was going and what they were doing. As they ran into issues, they first scrutinized them according to the word of God, then charted a path forward that bridged major cultural impasses using the culture of the word (Acts 15:1–34).

Contextualization

Effective evangelists, catechists, pastors, and teachers are sensitive to their social context. Just as the apostles in the church's early years, we use the language and vernacular of the people we're working with. In order to speak the gospel viscerally and clearly, we need to be aware of contemporary cultural pressures and social trends. This has been true for the church's mission in every era. This is simply common sense. Mission looks different in every era because culture is always shifting. Like foliage on a tree it changes every season. But the word of God alone nourishes Christ's church; the word is the deep roots of mission.

Christians are aliens and pilgrims in this fallen world; like Abraham, we pursue a city with foundations "whose designer and builder is God" (Heb 11:10). Rather than settling into the fading accommodations of a collapsing cultural context, the church seeks a lasting home in God's eternally transcendent word and the culture it grows. Context does not subsume the text of God. Context is the bridge between Christians and those who are lost sheep.

Textualization

The text of Scripture remains central in every context. That's how it was for the Jewish pilgrims so long ago in Jerusalem. Three thousand who heard Peter preach Jesus Christ and him crucified that Pentecost day believed, were baptized, and added to the church (Acts 2:41). Christians in every age and every place have much to learn from the mission template of that first congregation in Jerusalem.

The very heart and center of their life was God's word (Acts 2:42). The word of God (the apostles' teaching) was the source of their communion and unity (fellowship) nurtured in the Lord's Supper (the breaking of bread) and expressed in corporate liturgy (prayers). The life-giving power of the Holy Spirit in his living word shaped their thoughts, informed their behavior, directed their prayers, and gave them identity and vibrancy to face a brazenly decadent world very much like ours with confidence and hope. As a result, the Lord daily added to their number those who were being saved (2:47).

Under the Holy Spirit's blessing, that first Christian congregation's commonsense contextualization of God's word built a transcendent fellowship of believers extending out from the inhabitants of Jerusalem to the far-flung corners of the empire and beyond, just as Jesus had foretold: "But you will receive power when the Holy Spirit has come upon you, and you will be my witnesses in Jerusalem and in all Judea and Samaria, and to the end of the earth" (Acts 1:8).

This same mission continues today. By the power of the Holy Spirit working through his word, persons from every language, people, and tribe are being woven into God's own uniquely transcendent and eternal culture—a church that is one, holy, and truly catholic (or universal) (Eph 4:5–6).

Creating such a church—simultaneously contextual and universal—is admittedly challenging in a confused and chaotic world. But the culture of the word does the humanly impossible by the grace of God, bringing order out of chaos. As the word is sown, the culture is grown.

CHAPTER 3

The Church Proclaims Christ Jesus

Then Peter, filled with the Holy Spirit, said to them, "Rulers of the people and elders, if we are being examined today concerning a good deed done to a crippled man, by what means this man has been healed, let it be known to all of you and to all the people of Israel that by the name of Jesus Christ of Nazareth, whom you crucified, whom God raised from the dead—by him this man is standing before you well."

Acts 4:8–10

The culture of the word centers around the person of Jesus and his care for souls—the lost and the found, the sick and the well, the religious and irreligious, those near and far away. During Jesus's earthly ministry, the Gospels recorded his innate spiritual power and the keen insight he had into the souls around him. Caring for souls remained a focus for the New Testament church, and it is central today for mission work. What makes this focus so efficacious is the one who stands at the center of the culture of the word—the incarnate Word himself.

When Peter and John were interrogated by the authorities about their miraculous healing of a lame man in the temple, Peter boldly confessed concerning Jesus: "There is salvation in no one else, for there is no other name under heaven given among men by which we must be saved" (Acts 4:12). All through history Christ Jesus has been the center of the church's life:

> Long ago, at many times and in many ways, God spoke to our fathers by the prophets, but in these last days he has spoken to us by his Son, whom he appointed the heir of all things, through whom also he created the world. (Heb 1:1–2)

Everything the Son accomplished for us and for our salvation by his cross and resurrection is now distributed in his word and received by means of the power and presence of his Holy Spirit (John 16:13–15). Mission begins with the person of Jesus.

But who is this Jesus? The real significance of Jesus often eludes people. Many consider him a killjoy—just another ancient moralist. Others see him as an exemplary first-century activist or effective life coach. There's much misunderstanding about Jesus's true identity.

The first disciples of Jesus were confused too. Jesus taught them for the better part of three years about who he was and what he came to earth to do, yet even on the verge of his ascension they were still looking for him to launch an earthly kingdom (Acts 1:6). Instead, Jesus pointed them to the outpouring of the Holy Spirit and their ensuing mission: "But you will receive power when the Holy Spirit has come upon you, and you will be my witnesses in Jerusalem and in all Judea and Samaria, and to the end of the earth" (1:8). After the Holy Spirit opened their ears and eyes, they began to grasp the full significance of his redeeming work as both God and man.

Jesus Forgives Sins

Throughout his earthly ministry, Jesus did what only God could do. One day, in the shadow of the temple, the scribes and Pharisees publicly presented Jesus with a quandary: "Teacher, this woman has been caught in the act of adultery. Now in the

Law, Moses commanded us to stone such women. So what do you say?" (John 8:4–5).

Amazingly Jesus didn't answer, but stooping down, he began to write in the dirt with his finger. When they kept badgering him, he got up and calmly said, "Let him who is without sin among you be the first to throw a stone at her." Then he bent down and continued writing (John 8:7–8).

One by one the religious experts vanished until only Jesus was left with the woman standing alone before him. He stood up and addressed her again, "'Woman, where are they? Has no one condemned you?' She said, 'No one, Lord.' And Jesus said, 'Neither do I condemn you; go, and from now on sin no more' " (John 8:10–11). Though the Pharisees and scribes had been ready to punish her sin with death, Jesus sent her home freed from both sin's guilt and power.

Jesus's compassion and cross always go together. Broken people long for mercy and compassion. They may not be able to recite every one of God's commandments, but they sense sin's impact through personal guilt. They may not have learned of God's impending judgment in church, but they endure vindictive cruelty from their peers. They may not exactly repent of their sins, but they face the consequences of sin every time they see a loved one lying in a casket or when they confront mortality in terms of their own failing health. The Jesus who bore the cross is full of compassion for social misfits and broken hearts. Jesus forgives sins to save souls.

Jesus the God/Man

Jesus drew the Pharisees' indignation because of his avowal "before Abraham was, I am" (John 8:58). "I Am" is the divine name God revealed to Moses (Exod 3:14). By claiming God's holy name for himself, they thought Jesus had committed blasphemy. So, they picked up stones to kill him. Jesus eluded them and slipped out of the temple (John 8:59). Some days later, a trial was held and the Jewish people had their say. After Pilate acquitted Jesus of any capital crime under Roman law, they countered, "We have a law, and according to that law he ought to die because he has made himself the Son of God" (19:7).

So, who is Jesus? By his own actions and testimony, Jesus is God in human flesh. He forgave sins, as with the adulterous woman. He claimed God's holy name for himself, affirming himself as God's own Son. Yet he is not God pretending to be human; he is as fully human as any other person.

"God from God, light from light and very God from very God" the early church called Jesus.[16] It is mind-boggling that God could visit planet earth in the person of a man. Yet on the basis of the holy Scriptures the church confesses Jesus as not only God but truly and completely human at the same time. "Who ... came down from heaven and was incarnate by the Holy Spirit of the virgin Mary and was made man."[17] One man but two natures. God wrapped up in human flesh.

"How will this be?" asked Mary after being told by the heavenly messenger that she was to bear a child (Luke 1:34). But this miracle was more than just a virgin conception. "The Holy Spirit will come upon you, and the power of the Most High will overshadow you; therefore the child to be born will be called holy—the Son of God" (1:35). There are three miracles in Christmas, Martin Luther observed: that a virgin would conceive; that God would become man; and that the human heart would believe it.[18]

The mission of the holy Christian church revolves around these three miracles. As astonishing as it is that a woman could conceive a baby without a man, it's more amazing still that God actually walked planet earth in the human flesh of Jesus of Nazareth. It's astounding that three days after he was put to death on a cross he was raised back to life again. Even more miraculously, God effectively still works spiritual virgin births in everyone who comes to faith: "But to all ... who believed in his name, he gave the right to become children of God, who were born, not of blood nor of the will of the flesh nor of the will of man, but of God" (John 1:12–13).

The Care of Souls

Jesus Christ is the great physician of souls. He employed both his human and divine natures for the care and cure of embodied souls, freeing them from addiction to sin and captivity to death. In Acts we see how Peter and John boldly carried on this ministry amid a chaotic world hostile to the gospel:

> When they were released, they went to their friends and reported what the chief priests and the elders had said to them. And when they heard it, they lifted their voices together to God and said … "Lord, look upon their threats and grant to your servants to continue to speak your word with all boldness, while you stretch out your hand to heal, and signs and wonders are performed through the name of your holy servant Jesus." (Acts 4:23–24a, 29–30)

Jesus is both the treatment and the health provider. He is simultaneously the cure for sin and the curate of the soul by means of his healing word. Once the complex causes of distress are identified, they can be treated with the life-giving word of Christ.[19] Compassionate soul care skills are as integral for evangelism and ministry in today's shifting culture as they were in the ministry of Jesus and his apostles in the budding New Testament church.

In the cultural swirl of our post-Christendom world, suffering humanity still needs the healing that Christ Jesus brings to wounded hearts and fractured souls. In the Gospels, we see Jesus at work cleansing broken hearts and healing aching souls.

Defilement

Some of the most vivid episodes of Jesus's healing are found in Luke's Gospel. One day as Jesus was on his way to tend to the gravely ill daughter of a synagogue ruler (Luke 8:40–42), among the crowd pressing around him was a woman suffering from chronic menstrual bleeding. Her embarrassing condition was desperate, for according to Mosaic law, it left her in a perpetual state of spiritual uncleanness. Mark notes that she had "suffered much under many physicians, and had spent all that she had, and was no better but rather grew worse" (Mark 5:26). Anyone chronically ill can sympathize.

But this woman's spiritual defilement was even more critical; it left her utterly devastated and despairing. Note that Jesus didn't isolate himself from this social outcast and spiritual outsider. With his purifying touch he sanctified her uncleanness, even though such physical contact defiled him spiritually in turn. Her healing was holistic. With his cleansing word Jesus simultaneously healed her bodily ailment and cleansed her spiritual defilement. Reaching across the social and spiritual chasm between them, Jesus restored her directly and tenderly: "Daughter, your faith has made you well; go in peace" (Luke 8:48).

Jesus's healing word touches desperate people even today. It heals both body and soul, bringing cleansing and renewal. Cleansed and renewed by God's word, a company of sinners forms the culture of the word, which holds forth Jesus's healing word to fellow sinners. As the word is sown, the culture is grown.

Jesus also deliberately defiled himself in a literal brush with death. Luke records that as Jesus and his disciples were approaching the city gate of Nain, they encountered a funeral procession: "Behold, a man who had died was being carried out, the only son of his mother, and she was a widow, and a considerable crowd from the town was with her" (Luke 7:12). It was a pitiful sight. Not only was this grieving mother burying her only son, but previously she had lost her husband, leaving her with no evident support or care for her old age. No wonder she was accompanied by a "considerable crowd" of mourners.

Luke paints a poignant picture. Jesus, deeply moved by this grieving mother's tears, tenderly said, "Do not weep" (7:13). But his words were more than a polite social reflex; Jesus actually gave her a reason to stop crying.

Shockingly, Jesus reached out to touch the bier on which the young man's body rested. According to Mosaic law, anyone other than immediate family who willfully touched a dead body defiled their personal holiness (Num 19:11). In the Gospels we see similar incidents all throughout the ministry of Jesus. Everywhere Jesus went he absorbed sin and all its bitter consequences. He deliberately took onto himself and into himself not just the guilt of sin but all the defilement and shame of suffering humanity.

During the funeral procession that day, Jesus unraveled the power of death itself by the transformational power of his word. Turning from the woman, he directly addressed the corpse: "Young man, I say to you, arise" (Luke 7:14). As he would burst the bonds of death on Easter morn and as he shall call all the dead from their graves at the end of time, Jesus's words at Nain summoned life from death. "And the dead man sat up and began to speak, and Jesus gave him to his mother" (7:15).

Christ's powerful word is efficacious. It does what it says. It even conquers death itself. In the book of Acts, Luke documents how Jesus's healing ministry continued throughout the early church's mission, growing the culture of the word despite a hostile cultural context. After persecution broke out in Jerusalem,

> Philip went down to the city of Samaria and proclaimed to them the Christ. And the crowds with one accord paid attention to what was being said by Philip, when they heard him and saw the signs that he did. For unclean spirits, crying out with a loud voice, came out of many who had them, and many who were paralyzed or lame were healed. So there was much joy in that city. (Acts 8:5–8)

In a world filled with sorrow and heartache, such joy is desperately needed.

The Word in Action

That's how God's mission for the care of souls works in this sad world of ours, so filled with decay and death. We may sow in tears, but our hearts reap true joy from the pure joy-giver. Christ Jesus, his saving cross, and his dynamic word remain at the heart of mission today. This is the culture of the word in action, healing body, mind, and spirit. Broken bodies and suffering souls crave exactly what we've been given to bring them in Jesus's name.

The task of mission and evangelization in our neo-pagan world today is exactly as it was in the pagan world of the first apostles and evangelists: to rescue and to save people by the word of the gospel accompanied by deeds of love. The culture of this word brings renewal and hope because God's word always does what it says. The word of Christ Jesus crucified and risen heals holistically: it erases guilt, eradicates shame, and mends illnesses of both body and soul.

The woman caught in an act of adultery was freed from her guilt by Jesus's absolving word. The woman with the physical flow of blood was not only healed of her ailment but cleansed of her spiritual defilement by the touch of God's word made flesh. The grieving widow was consoled and handed resurrection joy. Today, suffering souls everywhere find life and healing within the fellowship of Christ's church. And these souls are embodied souls. In the compassionate care of souls in Jesus's name, needs of body, mind, and spirit are all addressed.

The care of souls is a two-step process: attention and intention. It involves both diagnosis and treatment.

Jesus the Diagnostician

One day a young man asked Jesus: "Good Teacher, what must I do to inherit eternal life?" (Luke 18:18). He claimed he had kept the second table of the law scrupulously, managing to avoid murder, adultery, theft, and false witness entirely. What's more, he claimed, he had always honored his father and mother (18:20).

It sounded good, but a great doctor probes for the disease lurking behind presenting symptoms. Jesus put his finger on this eager young man's foundational issue. "One thing you lack" (18:23), Jesus told him. Behind all that ethical zeal of his lay an idolatrous heart; he had the wrong god. His wealth and possessions were the source of his security and identity. Jesus outed that god: "Sell all you have and distribute to the poor ... and come, follow me" (18:22). It was a radical prescription, to be sure. But this man needed to eradicate his idol in order to truly live. His possessions had begun to take over his heart, leaving him in a deadly position.

The Idolatry Cure

The cure for certain death is Jesus. Those who confess the Lord Jesus as well as those who do not yet know him can find their life and health in the Lord who bought them with his blood.

The twofold remedy of repentance and forgiveness of sins is just what the doctor ordered for all the lambs and sheep of Christ Jesus, whether already in the flock or not yet gathered in (John 10:16).

Repentance and forgiveness compose God's two-pronged cure for idolatry. Both the turning away from sin and the cleansing from guilt flow from God's gifts, not the intentions of the human will. Jesus prescribed two things for the young man's mortal illness: giving up some of his wealth for the benefit of people in need (repentance) and following him (the forgiven life). Jesus offered him healing by these gifts, but sadly, he was not ready to receive them. He preferred his false god of wealth to the true God, the maker of heaven and earth.

When you introduce lost souls to God's efficacious word, some repent and believe; others don't. Ananias and Sapphira learned that the hard way. They willfully and deceitfully held back money for themselves after selling some property they had agreed to donate to the church. Peter confronted each of them, asking, "Why has Satan filled your heart to lie to the Holy Spirit?" (Acts 5:3, see also v. 9). The startling result was their instantaneous deaths because of their deceit and idolatry. The resulting fear that descended upon the whole church (5:5, 11) dramatically underscored just what's at stake in the care of souls and why the culture of the word is so important.

To cultivate the culture of the word, you speak the word and then step back and watch the Spirit go to work. You announce and reannounce the gospel, but the Holy Spirit does the rest.[20] In this way, more and more people hear the word and soul transformation takes place.

Gaining a Hearing

While apologetics and logical argumentation can help remove intellectual obstacles to the gospel, they no longer carry the weight they once did when human reason prevailed over private emotion and the church held a culturally privileged position.[21] Emotion and impulse have become the arbiters of truth.[22] In this new era, Christianity has negative connotations. As former cultural neutrality morphs into overt hostility toward Christian faith and life, traditional logic-based apologetics lose traction in witnessing, and spiritual dimensions loom larger.

The shift in morality and the rise of the digital age have radically altered the overall disposition of the human soul.[23] The main barrier to the faith has become more spiritual than cognitive. Therefore, Christian witness would do better not to begin with rational arguments for the faith but to apply the cleansing, healing, restoring, and identity-creating power of Christ and his word—and after that, its truth and reasonableness. As the world becomes increasingly toxic and lethal to sound bodies and souls, the church needs to dust off its classic heritage of the care and cure of souls with its attention to the diagnosis and treatment of spiritual ailments.[24]

Holistic Soul Care

Good medical doctors receive training in how to diagnose and treat chronic and acute illnesses. They seek to address the actual disease(s), not just the symptoms. They may prescribe some combination of medications, diet, exercise, and physical or mental regimens to bring the greatest possible degree of health to patients suffering physically, mentally, or emotionally. Physicians of the soul operate in a parallel way by means of God's word.

People today are suffering and in desperate need of comprehensive care, like the mugging victim in Jesus's parable (Luke 10:30–37). Stripped naked by robbers, he was beaten and left half dead in a ditch until a Samaritan happened along, treated his wounds, and then took care of him. "You go and do likewise," urges Jesus (10:37).

This is a call to action in a traumatized and fractured world. Christians need to step out of their comfort zones to bring Christ's healing to suffering souls. The priest and the Levite in the parable recoiled when they happened upon the bloodied victim lying at the roadside; they passed by on the other side.

We can all sympathize. At first glance some people do seem repulsive—too unpleasant to bother with. Many are victims of racism, poverty, and other social ills, suffering from hidden mental or emotional dysfunctions. They might not be "our kind" of person. They might not look like us. They could be mentally ill, suffering from extreme anxiety or depression. Maybe they are addicts or victims of sex trafficking. On the other hand, they could be dealers, traffickers, or sexual abusers. Yet none are beyond rescue and remedy. All are made in the image and likeness of God and equally beloved. Jesus shed his blood to cleanse, redeem, and heal them all. Like sheep without a shepherd, they wander lost and forlorn, drifting along empty and abandoned—without God and without hope in this world (Eph 2:12).

Christ's Remedy

The despised Samaritan intervened across cultural barriers to rescue and save a man deemed unworthy by spiritual elites. The Christian church in every age has been entrusted with the medicine of heaven for all types of human suffering. For souls impossibly weighed down by guilt or fouled in the filth of their own sin, there's release and freedom in the blood of Jesus that cleanses every sin (1 John 1:7). For souls oppressed and deeply wounded by the sins of others, there is a whole new life of hope and freedom. Freed from a crippling cycle of shame, remorse, and self-loathing, they find a place of honor among the saints and members of the very household of God himself (Eph 2:19).

The challenge is to pay attention and take action, like Jesus with hurting people, or like the Samaritan who reached out to care for the broken and battered man, or like Philip going to the Samaritans (Acts 8:5) and the Christians who went to the Greeks in Antioch (Acts 11:20). Many around us are the walking wounded, not just those walking into our church buildings on Sunday but people living and working in our communities and companies each and every day of the week. It's not enough to be attentive to spiritual casualties on Sundays and then bypass them every other day of the week. We're called to active engagement with suffering humanity each and every day. This means growing comfortable with being uncomfortable. The messiness of sin-afflicted lives, including ours, is not always pleasant to see or hear. Yet, since our Lord took upon himself our own mess, we need not be afraid to get a little messy as we bring him into the lives of others. The culture of the word embraces broken hearts and broken lives and transforms them in Christ Jesus.

Remedy of the Word

Confident mission in our time is rooted in the culture of the transcendent and transforming word of God. The culture of the word spreads as God's word is not only proclaimed by pastors but shared by all baptized believers and embodied in their daily lives. Not all Christians are called to be ministers in Christ's church, but every Christian bears witness to his word. Women and men alike can speak God's life-giving word to the walking wounded everywhere around them in this dark world, bringing help and healing in Jesus's name. By their words and deeds, they are the aroma of life and hope in a world reeking of doom and death (2 Cor 2:15–16).

Spiritual ruin and wreckage hem us in on every side. This world's culture lies in apparent shambles. The comfortable predictabilities of decades past are long gone. Yet the same Lord who sustained his church as she confronted the pagan world of antiquity beckons us forward into the tumultuous years ahead, guiding us by his sure word. "In the world you will have tribulation," said Jesus. "But take heart; I have overcome the world" (John 16:33).

A Fresh Vision

Rather than shrinking from the mess and chaos all around us, we need to see the world for what it is—created by God and ransomed by his Son. Rather than avoiding a collapsing culture and the spiritual zombies who populate it, it's time to take another look through the eyes of Jesus:

> When he saw the crowds, he had compassion for them, because they were harassed and helpless, like sheep without a shepherd. Then he said to his disciples, "The harvest is plentiful, but the laborers are few; therefore pray earnestly to the Lord of the harvest to send out laborers into his harvest." (Matt 9:36–38)

Granted, the task *is* overwhelming. It's far too big a job for any one of us. But we're not alone. Our Lord gave all his mission commands in the plural. Individually we may struggle and falter, but together we will win in the end: "Those who sow in tears shall reap with shouts of joy!" (Ps 126:5), and "the sufferings of this present time are not worth comparing with the glory that is to be revealed to us" (Rom 8:18). Christ's holy church will never ever perish, as Jesus himself said: "The gates of hell will not prevail against it" (Matt 16:18).

Christ Jesus has equipped his church for this very time by his word and Spirit. We gather together each Lord's Day to pray, speak, hear, and receive the Spirit in God's word. There Jesus incrementally builds his church of living stones to become a living temple where God is worshiped by his Spirit (1 Pet 2:5). The worshiping community is where his transforming word is sown. It remains the heart and center of the cultivation of a culture of the word for every passing era. As the word is sown, the culture is grown.

CHAPTER 4

The Church's Worship Transcends Cultural Context

While they were worshiping the Lord and fasting, the Holy Spirit said, "Set apart for me Barnabas and Saul for the work to which I have called them." Then after fasting and praying they laid their hands on them and sent them off.

Acts 13:2–3

From the inception of the New Testament church, worship has been central in the life of the church. After Pentecost, the word and its resulting culture was nurtured and fostered among the first disciples as they devoted themselves to "the apostles' teaching and the fellowship, to the breaking of bread and the prayers" (Acts 2:42). In every generation since, worship has been at the core of Christian mission and life.

Recent debates over screens, praise bands, and worship rites (ancient or contemporary) threaten to obscure the heart of the matter. Christian worship is a unique culture set in motion by the word. It is a prime expression of the culture of the word. The very first Christian congregation rooted their worship in the word, which included preaching, communion, and united prayer. So today, Christians assemble not merely to encourage each other or profess to God his greatness but to hear his word, eat the Lord's Supper, and pray corporately. This worship sows the word in a spoken and sacramental way. Once it takes root, the word works to enliven and protect, direct and correct our day-to-day lives as we live them out.

Worship involves both giving and receiving, but the receiving precedes the giving. Worship is the reciprocal connection between our loving God and his beloved people. It's been that way from the dawn of creation.

Dialogue with God

Since the beginning of time, God has been in continual dialogue with his people. In the garden of Eden, Adam and Eve communed with God; first they listened to his word, and then they responded by speaking with him. The first and most tragic consequence of their rebellion was a disruption in that life-giving conversation. When God came walking through the garden in the cool of the day, instead of running to meet him as they normally would, Adam and Eve hid from his presence. But though they fled from him, God's love still sought them. The Lord God called out to Adam, "Where are you?" (Gen 3:9), and he's been looking for his children ever since.

Our first parents were designed to worship. They were made for communion with God. They needed to hear his word and respond in kind, and they sustained their life by eating the fruit from the tree of life. That pattern for worship—hearing, speaking, and eating—governs Christian worship still today. It's what animates the culture of the word.

Worship and Culture

As the foremost among all God's creatures, Adam and Eve showed him honor and reverence by obeying the word of his command not to eat from the tree he had forbidden: "Of the tree of the knowledge of good and evil you shall not eat, for in the day that you eat of it you shall surely die" (Gen 2:17).

We demonstrate our reverence for God in different ways. Honoring God deserves our praise—the praise of all creation, in fact. "All your works shall give thanks to you, O Lord, and all your saints shall bless you" (Ps 145:10). We demonstrate our reverence for God in different ways. While worship is cultural because it necessarily uses the many different languages and diverse customs of the humans involved, at the same time it is transcultural. In worship, form follows function. Although our worship happens in this world, it's an otherworldly experience. Its content establishes its context; heaven comes down to earth. God condescends to dwell on earth among his people by means of the preaching of his gospel and the administration of his sacraments.

God shows up wherever his word is preached (Matt 18:20). And God's word always does what it says (Isa 55:10–11). So, God's word and God's presence always go together. This is what makes the word so powerful: He's always present in the culture grown by his word.

Worship happens whenever God reaches into our time and space by his word to bring us his forgiveness, and then we respond in prayer and praise. The best worship forms and rituals are not empty cultural gestures or obscure formalities. Instead, rooted in the efficacious word of God, holy rites enact invisible spiritual realities.

For example, when Moses met God at the burning bush on Mt. Horeb, he was instructed to take off his shoes, "for the place on which you are standing is holy ground" (Exod 3:5). Removing his sandals was ritual behavior, to be sure, but no mere formality. It was the way Moses showed he had come into contact with the living God by means of his word. Though unseen, God was present there, triggering this extraordinary response. This exemplifies how worship and culture intersect; the cultural setting determines the way the worshiper responds to the power of the word. Worship is the word of God enacted.

Ordinary behavior is inappropriate in extraordinary situations. The presence of God calls for suitable reverence. Over the centuries the church has developed a liturgy rooted in the conviction that God is actually present wherever two or more Christians are gathered to hear the word of Jesus and partake of his body and blood in the supper he instituted the night of his betrayal. "For as often as you eat this bread and drink the cup, you proclaim the Lord's death until he comes" (1 Cor 11:26).

Worship anticipates the life to come (Heb 12:22–24) while remaining contemporary (in that it happens in the present), being rooted in the past, and extending forward into eternity. It connects us to Jesus in exalted glory and to the saints and angels worshiping even now in heaven's glory. Word-based worship is simultaneously contextual and textual, both cultural and transcultural. At first this kind of worship may seem awkward to our contemporaries, but it transforms precisely because it is transcendent.

Bridging Time and Space

Because worship is transcendent, you might also call it countercultural. We live in a fixed, three-dimensional physical world with the spiritual dimension often not making the noticeboard.

Worship rooted in God's Spirit-filled word counters the constraints of our existence by opening up the realm of the Spirit to flesh-and-blood humans. There's a connection between what happens in every church on Sunday mornings, what happened among the first believers in Jerusalem, and what will happen as seen in John's visionary experience of Revelation so long ago in his exile on Patmos. All these experiences revolve around the presence of Jesus in his living word. The unseen reality behind genuine Christian worship is the presence of the living Lord Jesus and all his saints in glory, enacted by the word of God.

In a religious climate where many—especially the young—are captivated by things ethereal and spiritual, we should deliberately connect our worship practices more with the transcendent culture of the word. Worship patterns and customs can be evaluated in this regard with a few key questions: Is our way of worship in harmony with what Jesus gave to his church on earth initially and what his church in heaven will be doing for all eternity? Is our worship practice a wall or a window? Does it draw attention to itself, the worship leaders, and the worshiping assembly? Or, in contrast, is it a window into the unseen realm where God pours out his gifts by means of his word and Spirit? In our worship are we catering to self-indulgence or pointing to God's grace in Christ Jesus? Our persistent aim should be to become less and less focused on our earthly assembly and more and more conscious of our Lord and his saints already worshiping around his throne in glory. Worship is done so the word can be sown and its culture grown, not so that stylistic preferences can be sown and their market share grown.

In a humble gathering on Patmos amid his fellow worshipers, John experienced heaven on earth. He glimpsed saints and angels in heaven's eternal glory actively joining in their earthly worship. He saw God seated on his throne. In the foreground stood Jesus, the Lamb of God, slain for the sins of the world before time began (Rev 13:8) but now alive forevermore. Four "living creatures" (the whole created universe) and twenty-four "elders" (the church of the Old and New Testaments) joined in joyous praise of Jesus for his saving work.

> And when he had taken the scroll, the four living creatures and the twenty-four elders fell down before the Lamb, each holding a harp, and golden bowls full of incense, which are the prayers of the saints. And they sang a new song, saying,
>
> "Worthy are you to take the scroll
> and to open its seals,
> for you were slain, and by your blood you ransomed
> people for God
> from every tribe and language and people and nation,
> and you have made them a kingdom and priests
> to our God,
> and they shall reign on the earth."
>
> Then I looked, and I heard around the throne and the living creatures and the elders the voice of many angels,

> numbering myriads of myriads and thousands of thousands, saying with a loud voice,
>
> "Worthy is the Lamb who was slain,
> to receive power and wealth and wisdom and might
> and honor and glory and blessing!" (Rev 5:8–12)

This description of the word actively enacted in heaven lifts up our hearts from earthly matters to these heavenly realities. Worship here on earth prepares us for the culmination of worship in glory.

Church Attendance

For now, worshipers gather in traditional sanctuaries, modern megachurches, living rooms, or in some places around the world, thatched-roof shelters or secret enclaves to avoid persecution. Numbers range from a handful of people to thousands. The majority of churches in America average less than one hundred people in attendance.[25]

Admittedly, those numbers are concerning. For decades church membership has been declining, falling, and failing. We can't just turn our backs on this information and hope for the best. Vacant pews and aging congregants are trending in American congregations. Despite seven decades of emphasis on outreach and mission, numbers continue to plummet. A variety of solutions have been tried.

One attempted remedy has been to contextualize worship and mission, as though by tweaking the church's message and methodology it can attract an increasingly disinterested public. Church doesn't seem to work any longer, so church leaders and evangelists keep on trying to remodel the church in the image of the culture. But as the culture moves beyond postmodern to post-Christian, that approach becomes increasingly problematic. We're not evangelizing the culture, but the people who live within ever-shifting cultures. A better approach is to adopt the apostolic church's model, where the text of Scripture takes priority over the cultural context. The earliest chapter in the church's history points us to the word as the source of her life and vitality.

No matter the setting, worship sets forth the word and its saving power. Word-centered worship was the core of apostolic mission throughout the book of Acts, as it was in Philippi:

> And on the Sabbath day we went outside the gate to the riverside, where we supposed there was a place of prayer, and we sat down and spoke to the women who had come together. One who heard us was a woman named Lydia, from the city of Thyatira, a seller of purple goods, who was a worshiper of God. The Lord opened her heart to pay attention to what was said by Paul. And after she was baptized, and her household as well, she urged us, saying, "If you have judged me to be faithful to the Lord, come to my house and stay." And she prevailed upon us. (Acts 16:13–15)

Whether preached in the open air, as Paul did in Philippi, or in private houses as the apostles and evangelists did in other locales, the word of the Lord took root everywhere it was shared, producing fruits of faith and love among those who heard throughout the Mediterranean world. First the word of God is sown, then that word grows its own transforming culture.

The Presence of Jesus

What gave the word its transcultural power was the presence of Jesus. For wherever his word is, there is Jesus. The first Christians saw God's word as the beating heart of their life together and their interactions with an unbelieving world. The pattern initially laid down in Jerusalem was replicated everywhere the gospel spread throughout the Mediterranean. Christians depended on Christ Jesus for life here and eternally. As the body of Christ daily at work in his name in a pagan culture, they drew their nurture and vitality from the culture of the word enacted in their worshiping assembly each Lord's Day—with Jesus at the center. After Paul's conversion, his gospel mission to Jew and gentile alike followed the Jerusalem worship model: apostolic teaching, prayer, and the breaking of the bread (Acts 20:7).

The peace of Christ and his vivifying word were not just explored in sermon and song. Christ Jesus himself was invisibly present among them as they gathered in his name, as Paul reminded the congregation in Colossae:

> Put on then, as God's chosen ones, holy and beloved, compassionate hearts, kindness, humility, meekness, and patience, bearing with one another and, if one has a complaint against another, forgiving each other; as the Lord has forgiven you, so you also must forgive. And above all these put on love, which binds everything together in perfect harmony. And let the peace of Christ rule in your hearts, to which indeed you were called in one body. And be thankful. Let the word of Christ dwell in you richly, teaching and admonishing one another in all wisdom, singing psalms and hymns and spiritual songs, with thankfulness in your hearts to God. And whatever you do, in word or deed, do everything in the name of the Lord Jesus, giving thanks to God the Father through him. (Col 3:12–17)

Just as the early church's worship revolved around the presence of Jesus, so it does today. Because Christ Jesus promises to be present by means of his word to bring forgiveness and life, his life-giving word shapes all preaching, praying, and singing. In every cultural context through the ages, the culture of the word breaks every barrier to transform hearts and lives.

Something Old and Something New

Through the ages the church has borrowed and adapted elements from each passing culture without selling herself to any one era. In her music, for example, she borrows tunes, tonalities, and instruments from multiple genres and ethnicities. Yet she never merely copies pop culture. In her worship the church is not some pale imitation of secular entertainment styles, but she rises above it to lift the hearts and eyes of worshipers to sacred and transcendent realities.

Like a great coral reef, the contemporary church's worship is built on skeletons of ancient organisms. She is no custodian of dead traditions, however, but the stewardess of the faith once delivered to the saints (Jude 1:3). The customs of each generation organically connect with worship forms from past generations, still giving life today in the precious souls of people ransomed out from every nation and language and tribe by the blood of Jesus to be a kingdom of priests to his God and Father (Rev 1:5–6).

The church's contemporary communion and fellowship thus extend beyond time and space to encompass saints living and departed from every land and culture. Like the reef, her roots are in the depths of enduring tradition, but she lives in the present. She speaks the language of heaven with the accents of earth. In the gathered church, her earthly songs echo the praises resounding in eternal glory. She focuses not on amusement or entertainment but on God, his word, and the culture that goes with it.

The Entertainment Pitfall

The ancient world knew the power of spectacle. Adoring throngs in Rome celebrated the triumph of returning victorious legions with elaborate pageantry, games, and feasting. Public amphitheaters featured comedic and tragic dramas performed to the great delight and amusement of citizens in both small and large cities. The Caesars staged spectacular performances in Rome's Circus Maximus, featuring troupes of jugglers and entertainers and climaxing with the bloody sport of gladiatorial combat.

Early church leaders denounced these entertainments because they aroused sinful human passions—a cardinal principle in navigating the tension between cultural context and the culture of the word. Emotion for its own sake undermines the culture of the word. Spectacle overpowers the senses. As the New Testament church shows us, the purpose of worship is not to entertain, superficially attract, and overwhelm, but to hear God's word and praise his name as he comes among us with his gifts—chiefly the remission of sins in Jesus's blood.

As the Christian church grew from its humble roots as a persecuted minority into the prevailing religion throughout the Western world, its way of worship evolved significantly. Large churches accommodated thousands of worshipers at once, some taking on the appearance and style of government palaces. Worship services and pubic liturgies became more and more extravagant, enhanced by elaborate pageantry and ceremony. Periodically the church recognized a need for review as worship practices stretched the parameters of the word. This required liturgical correction and redirection. She paid particular attention to the relationship between the word and music in her worship.

Music and Worship

Unfortunately, worship songs have become somewhat blasé among Christians. This is largely because music in contemporary secular society has become mostly a consumer commodity. Several generations ago, people could only hear professional musicians in person. Modern digital technology enables them to carry their favorite tunes everywhere, plugged into personal earbuds or blasted on external speakers. We don't make music ourselves much anymore; we just listen to it passively.

In countless sanctuaries around the country the same phenomena can be heard—or not heard, to be more precise. Amplified soloists or choirs and praise bands perform songs that are either too complex or unfamiliar for the congregation to attempt, so they sit and listen, passively. The congregation then becomes an audience. Its focus is not on hearing and singing and praying the word of God but being entertained, despite worship leaders' best intentions.

Many good books address best practices in church music, so we won't explore this further.[26] The point is that the music itself is not the focus in worship but the means. Church music must be culturally authentic and contextually relevant, to be sure, but subservient to the word of God. If the focus is not on the word, the culture produced can only be of the world.

If music is all that matters, the resulting culture may be musically rich but empty of salvation.

The rich tapestry of Christian hymnody and song includes vastly different musical styles, ranging from elaborate renaissance choral polyphony, to the lilting harmonies of Scandinavia, to the sturdy pulsing sounds of the German chorale, to the call-and-response rhythmic music of Africa, to the soaring tonalities of English cathedrals, to the open harmonics of the Appalachian shape-note tradition, and much, much more. The church in her collective wisdom has harnessed a myriad of musical forms in faithful service to the text of God's word.

The worshiping church has been at her best when she sings the Lord's song (Ps 137:4) in ways that human ears can clearly hear the word of God, which is the core of that eternal song. Thus, the church uses the musical genres of each and every culture in which she lives (commonsense contextualization evaluated through holy discernment) to support one consistent transcendent song (the text of God's word). She seeks to weave her contemporary voice with saints of every time and place into one eternal song, which is simultaneously "the song of Moses, the servant of God, and the song of the Lamb" (Rev 15:3).

Worship Yesterday, Today, and Forever

Worship governed by the word has a certain direction and flow: from God to us and back again. At the heart of all worship stands Jesus, who is the great high priest in God's heavenly sanctuary (Heb 10:19–22). By his sacrificial death and resurrection, he has opened the kingdom of heaven to all believers. We trust in the promises of forgiveness, life, and salvation he has attached to his gracious commands: "Proclaim the gospel" (Mark 16:15); "Take, eat. … Drink" (Matt 26:26–27); "Go … baptizing them" (28:19). Consequently, Christian services include the word, prayer, and meals everywhere, echoing in various ways the pattern of worship Jesus first established. Even free-form worship gravitates toward some type of predictable structure or liturgy.

"Liturgy" originally meant a public service that Roman citizens provided for the greater good of the empire, such as building roads or public utilities.[27] Jesus, a citizen of the new Jerusalem, has offered all his goods—his very life—for the benefit of the whole world. In obedience to his commands and trusting in his promises the church continues to draw her life from him. The earliest forms of Christian worship were rooted in the prayer services of the synagogue, with the addition of apostolic teaching and the "breaking of the bread" or the Lord's Supper (Acts 2:42). Gradually the Lord's Prayer and other scriptural prayers were added, such as the Gloria (the song of the angels from Luke 2:14), the Sanctus (the hymn of the angels from Isa 6:3 plus the acclamation at Jesus's entry into Jerusalem from Matt 21:9), and the songs of Mary (Luke 1:46–55), Zechariah (1:68–79), Simeon (2:29–32), and others. The goal was to catechize the faithful in everything Jesus taught his disciples (Matt 28:20). Musical settings varied widely, of course, because they were contextual, but biblical texts governed what was sung. The word prevailed, and its culture grew.

These ancient worship songs filled with God's word are the heritage of all Christians, not just historically liturgical churches. Their fundamental texts distill the essence of the faith once delivered to the saints (Jude 1:3), training each Christian generation in the basic vocabulary of faith so they can all the more confidently confess with their lips what they believe in their hearts (Rom 10:9). Since its beginning, the church has taught young and old the central texts of faith, such as the Apostles' Creed, the Ten Commandments, and the Lord's Prayer. Imparting these key texts has become known as "catechesis"—the inculcation of God's word. As the word is sown in the hearts and lives of each generation, the culture of the word grows, bearing the fruit of faith in works of love and service.

Liturgical worship, far from a mere aesthetic experience, has been a life-giving tool for catechesis and evangelization over the centuries. Liturgical rites have morphed and changed with shifting locations and culture, but the one constant in worship has been the use of the words of Scripture itself in prayer and praise. Here's another great instance of common-sense contextualization supporting the culture of the word.

A scriptural liturgy is an essential tool for Christian mission today, just as it has been for two thousand years. It shows us how to read the Bible, how to pray, and how to live. It encourages consistently faithful testimony to Jesus despite opposing cultural winds. It sows the word and grows its culture. Whether simple or elaborate according to taste and custom, Christian worship connects the faithful to the heavenly liturgy of saints above and the myriad angels singing their eternal praises to the God of all creation.

Heaven on Earth

Our worship on earth is but a dim reflection of the real worship service going on eternally around God's throne in glory. Christians in every generation can take heart, knowing that in their earthly worship they're connected with that mighty throng gathered on another shore and in a brighter light. What you see in your local church is not the whole picture. The reality is much more profound:

> But you have come to Mount Zion and to the city of the living God, the heavenly Jerusalem, and to innumerable angels in festal gathering, and to the assembly of the firstborn who are enrolled in heaven, and to God, the judge of all, and to the spirits of the righteous made perfect, and to Jesus, the mediator of a new covenant, and to the sprinkled blood that speaks a better word than the blood of Abel. (Heb 12:22–24)

This heavenly vision shapes our worship assemblies even now in the face of mounting secularism and paganism in our society.

We need to consider how well our worship services reflect the heavenly worship above. Who is the subject of the verbs: you or God? What's going on in your worship—is it heaven on earth, singing the songs of Zion, or just another group of people telling God how they feel about him? Worship should focus on Jesus and his cross—what he has done and is doing for us—not what we're doing for him.

Although our citizenship is in heaven (Phil 3:20), we're not there yet. We live very much in the context of this world, even as we draw our life and sustenance from the word. Our place is heaven's outpost here on earth. Although we remain in the world, we are not of it. As the word is sown, its culture is grown.

CHAPTER 5

The Church Lives in the World, Not of the World

And Agrippa said to Paul, "In a short time would you persuade me to be a Christian?" And Paul said, "Whether short or long, I would to God that not only you but also all who hear me this day might become such as I am—except for these chains."

Acts 26:28–29

The apostle Paul embraced everything that came with following Christ, chains and all. The afflictions he endured for the sake of the gospel were many. They ran the full gamut from natural disasters to human opponents: shipwreck, dangers on sea and land, robbers, religious zealots and false teachers within and without the church, plus hunger and hardship in many arduous journeys (2 Cor 11:24–28).

Paul loved the Lord Jesus and the people to whom he ministered. He was alert to the opportunities to evangelize and confess Christ, as he did before King Agrippa. He understood what it was to be in the world, enduring all the heartache, temptations, and challenges that went with it. Yet he was not of the world. Since his conversion on the Damascus road, it became ever clearer to him that the personal costs were well worth it. Paul remained faithful in evangelizing the lost and shepherding the found, even to the point of death. His extraordinary passion and ability to endure such intense persecutions were not of his own doing. It flowed from his trust and confidence in Christ and his word: "For the sake of Christ, then, I am content with weaknesses, insults, hardships, persecutions, and calamities. For when I am weak, then I am strong" (2 Cor 12:10). The Lord Jesus had earlier prayed for such faithful endurance among all his disciples.

> I have given them your word, and the world has hated them because they are not of the world, just as I am

> not of the world. I do not ask that you take them out of the world, but that you keep them from the evil one. They are not of the world, just as I am not of the world. Sanctify them in the truth; your word is truth. As you sent me into the world, so I have sent them into the world." (John 17:14–18)

He prayed for Paul, in other words. But he also prayed for you. That night before his bitter suffering and agonizing death, he prayed not only for his beloved disciples but all those in the future who would believe in him through the word he left behind with them (John 17:20).

Word vs. World

But those words Jesus bequeathed to his church imperil us. He received them from his Father in heaven, and we draw our very life and being from them. Yet that life-giving word also places us under attack from the devil, world, and flesh. Just as the world hated Jesus because of the word he received from the Father, his disciples will be hated too.

That's our predicament today. The word of God upon which the church is built is abhorrent to the world. We can't talk intelligently about commonsense contextualization in worship and mission until we grasp that we live on a battlefield. The devil, the father of lies, remains the sworn enemy of God and his church in each and every era. Satan relentlessly targets the mission Jesus carries out by the word of his gospel.

The church's mission is therefore a balancing act. The world is precious to God. He made it in the beginning and then redeemed it by his beloved Son. But this world is enemy-occupied territory. It has been invaded by the prince of darkness, the evil one Jesus repeatedly warned against throughout his teaching. Satan uses anything and everything in this world to attack our faith and distract us from the word. Greed, power, lust, poverty, wealth, and status are a few of the tools he uses to pry us away from the truth of Christ and his saving word. He can even turn truth into misbelief, twisting such virtues as compassion, justice, and equity into destructive ideologies inimical to the faith. He's obsessed with undermining our faith and reliance on the word. Yet the very same word that's so repulsive to the world protects us from the evil one. Jesus prayed that his disciples would be preserved—even more, that they would be sanctified—by his word of truth: "Sanctify them in the truth; your word is truth" (John 17:17).

While the church seeks to be *in* the world, she is never *of* it. She is ever at war. Her battle is not political, philosophical, nor even, properly speaking, cultural. She's not seeking to convert the culture in which she lives but to convert the people living in each culture down through the ages. Her instrument is the word; she's sowing God's word and growing the culture of the word. Every era is continually pressured to derive their truth, values, and identity from the cultural context of this fallen world instead of the transformational word of God. That word, and the transcendent identity and distinct fruit it brings, bridges continents and people groups to create one church out of people from many diverse and divergent cultures.

Turning Things Upside Down

A careful reading of the New Testament record shows that people across vastly different cultures are simultaneously repelled and attracted by the faithful preaching of the word. The cross-centered gospel of Christ Jesus uproots and undermines idolatry in every cultural context, even as it ushers people into God's transcendent kingdom, not bound by time or space. Because it is countercultural, the word of God is transcultural.

Two striking examples of contextualized cross-cultural mission are recorded in Acts 17. The church in her infancy bridged two different cultural contexts—Thessalonica and Athens—using one and the same word.

Paul and Silas arrived in Thessalonica on the Greek peninsula, where Paul spent three Sabbaths in the local synagogue planting the word by using classic dialectical argumentation to demonstrate how the cross fit into God's plan of salvation. On the basis of Old Testament prophetic Scriptures, he proved that Jesus was the promised Messiah (Christ) of Israel and "that it was necessary for the Christ to suffer and to rise from the dead" (Acts 17:3). Paul's preaching gained a rich harvest. New Christian converts included some members of the synagogue as well as believing Greeks and a considerable number of prominent women in the city (17:4).

But his message didn't sit well with everyone. A local mob rallied against them. When Paul and Silas were nowhere to be found, the crowd went after the man who had sheltered them in his house. They dragged Jason and some of the new Christians before the city magistrates, accusing them of disturbing the peace: "These men who have turned the world upside down have come here also, and Jason has received them, and they are all acting against the decrees of Caesar, saying that there is another king, Jesus" (Acts 17:6–7). Clearly, there's something inherently offensive about the culture of the word. When it disrupts commonly held customs and cultural assumptions, it interrupts the world's agenda. In the ancient world, as now, the message regarding Christ crucified was problematic—a scandal to Jews and folly to gentiles (1 Cor 1:23).

The word of God upsets the world's equilibrium because it turns an unbelieving world and its culture upside down. When God becomes the center of life rather than personal desires and achievement, it impacts the way people live. New thoughts, a new identity, and a new way of life implant among them. That can be irritating to some. The word is countercultural.

Yet it's also transcultural, as we see when Paul left Thessalonica for Athens.

Expounding Something New

Paul began planting the word in Athens exactly as he did in Thessalonica; he reasoned with the Jews in their synagogue and in the city marketplace, preaching Jesus as the Messiah, crucified and risen. Philosophers of the Epicurean and Stoic schools took notice of what Paul was saying, and they wanted to hear more. So, they brought him to the Areopagus, a place for public dialectic on a hilltop near the Acropolis. The Acropolis was filled with religious shrines and temples, including the famed Parthenon that housed a colossal image of the goddess Athena. There they requested: "May we know what this new teaching is that you are presenting?" (Acts 17:19).

Paul's answer was the epitome of commonsense contextualization tempered by holy discernment. He showed great restraint in that pagan religious hotbed. Though there were idols everywhere and the elite of the city prided themselves on their religious ideas, he didn't call them the idolaters they were. Instead, he showed salutary adaptability and proceeded diplomatically:

> Men of Athens, I perceive that in every way you are very religious. For as I passed along and observed the objects of your worship, I found also an altar with this inscription: "To the unknown god." What therefore you worship as unknown, this I proclaim to you. (Acts 17:22–23)

Here we see God's word in action not in the context of a believing Jewish community but among pagan Greek philosophers. Paul proceeded to proclaim Christ crucified, but he began with natural revelation—what everyone can deduce on the basis of the created order. Then he paid tribute to the religious heritage of his hearers, even quoting classic Greek literature. Yet he didn't hesitate to get to the heart of the matter: how in the fullness of time God revealed himself in the person of his son Jesus the Christ, crucified and risen (Acts 17:31).

The preaching of Jesus's resurrection provoked different reactions. Some scoffed. Others were curious, saying they were open to hearing more. But some believed, including one prominent teacher among the Areopagus philosophers named Dionysius, a woman named Damaris, and others with them (Acts 17:34).

We see that the word of the Lord was planted and flourished in two radically different contexts: in the synagogue of Thessalonica among the Jews and on the Areopagus among the philosophers of Athens. The word can be sown across cultural barriers, bearing fruit in the lives of diverse people groups. Today, we're not striving to convert cultures but people living in diverse cultures.

The Transforming Word

Wherever the word takes root, it transforms people, restoring broken relationships. It gives new life individually and collectively. It changes hearts in every era, nation, and language, including abusive cultural contexts. In Britain and America, the word of God produced abolitionists who spoke against the evils of slavery. It forged a resistance network in Germany against the National Socialist Party agenda and in defense of their targeted Jewish victims, at considerable risk to personal safety. God's word still moves people today to defend the marginalized, the weak, and the unborn. The word generates hope and positive action in the face of a hostile world.

Christians are not intimidated when a secular or pagan culture finds the gospel offensive. They do not hide their faith under a bushel. They are not monks living in splendid spiritual isolation, shielded from the world around them. They daily interact with people whose values, habits, and beliefs are much at odds with their own. Like the earliest Christians, they remain very much *in* the world. Yet they are distinctively not *of* the world. As strangers and foreigners in a world estranged from God, their lives are demonstrably different from others around them.

> Beloved, I urge you as sojourners and exiles to abstain from the passions of the flesh, which wage war against your soul. Keep your conduct among the Gentiles honorable, so that when they speak against you as evildoers, they may see your good deeds and glorify God on the day of visitation. (1 Pet 2:11–12)

Witness

Christians are not escapists. They flee from sin but never from the world. It can be easy to bring an overreaction as a corrective to cultural trends. Withdrawal and isolation on the one hand or crusading and activism on the other are perennial temptations. Yet, Christians bring the word to bear on the various cultures of this world by living out their vocations in family, work, and community.[28] Christians are active, but they are not just another ideological activist group. They are present and engaged, sowing the word, living the word, cultivating the culture of the word.

Simple things—like a cup of water in Jesus's name—become significant. Changing a diaper, loading a trailer, drafting a report. Nothing flashy. By simply serving in their daily callings, Christians provide a powerful witness by what they say and do. To borrow images from Jesus, Christians are salt and light, providing both illumination and preservation in a dark and decaying world (Matt 5:14). Like leaven, they grow the kingdom slowly but steadily—stealthily, you could say—here in this world (Luke 13:20–21). *In* the world, yes. But ever and always *of* the word.

The word of God incrementally shapes believers—first ritually and sacramentally, then morally and ethically. It's like a seed that germinates, sprouts, takes root, grows up into a plant, and then bears fruit. God's word determines how Christians see their personal identity and being, their physical bodies, their vocations in family, work, church, and society. All these private and public aspects of their lives are shaped and enlivened by the living word of God.

The word of the Lord continues to grow in our midst just as it did among the first Christians. They made an impact on their world both individually and collectively. We can as well—but only by the power of the word.

As the bride of Christ in this world, the church is continually shaped and formed by his word. Until Jesus comes again, she remains steadfastly *in* this world but not *of* it. She derives her being and identity not from worldly cultures but the word of God. Robert Jenson outlines the stance of Christians toward cultural issues.

> So what, if anything, should the Church do about the state of Western culture? To deal cogently with that question, we must avoid an error that has confused much of the discussion. The question about "Christ and Culture," as if Christ were one sort of reality and culture simply another, has generated much admirable thought but is nevertheless a category mistake. For the Church is herself manifestly a culture, and according to the New Testament the Church is the embodiment of Christ. The question then should be about "Christ and Other Cultures."[29]

The church herself is a culture. She has a culture uniquely her own to which she welcomes individuals from every language, tribe, and people down through history. That culture grows *in* the world, but it is definitely not *of* the world. It's rooted firmly in the word, the word that has been speaking and creating ever since the dawn of time.

Living Counterculturally

Being *of* the world inevitably sabotages mission. Christians must ever be on their guard lest they capitulate to their passions and become people *of* the world. Left unexamined, material possessions, fame, and worldly achievements take over and begin to define us. They teach us to love things and use people rather than use things and love people. Paradoxically, the very technology we devise to enhance human life can make it more inhuman.

This is especially noticeable in the digital age. Social media designed to bring people together tends to drive them further apart. Digital devices invented to lighten human labor often add to our stress levels. But this is nothing new. Inevitably every innovative technology, be that the sixteenth-century printing press or twenty-first-century digital media, brings with it unintended consequences which call for careful examination in light of God's word.

God's unchanging word shines the clear beacon of truth on passing cultural trends. Expressive individualism seductively offers a universe of one's own creation, but God himself is the almighty maker of heaven and earth. Families are scornfully dismissed as relics of an old-fashioned repressive patriarchy, even though God lovingly inscribed in the bodies of our first parents the blessings of motherhood and fatherhood: "Be fruitful and multiply and fill the earth" (Gen 1:28). Destructive ideologies morph the sexual binary into an endless series of gender identities, whereas God explicitly created male and female as distinct expressions of his own image (Gen 1:27).[30] When the sexed body becomes a mere avatar of one's inner "self" something essential to human nature is irretrievably damaged.[31] Reproductive technologies see human embryos as manufactured commodities that can be assembled or discarded at will instead of the mysterious creation of God through the bodily union of a father and mother. When procreation is divorced from sex, humans pursue the orgasm of their private choice rather than giving themselves one to another in heterosexual marital union according to God's design (Gen 2:24).

Wherever unbridled expressive individualism holds sway, good and healthy human desires become destructive obsessive compulsions.

Freedom or Bondage?

The classical world of antiquity saw such an uninhibited pursuit of the passions not as freedom but slavery. The liberal arts were devised in that ancient pagan era in order to free people from neurotic bondage to their innermost desires. Virtuous living was prescribed as a way to free people. Aristotle's classic virtues were prudence, justice, temperance, and fortitude.[32]

Christians before Christendom upheld virtue as well, though of a different sort. They promoted a baptismal virtue rooted in Christ Jesus himself: "If the Son sets you free, you will be free indeed" (John 8:36). Being baptized with Jesus, buried along with him in his death, and raised again to lives governed by his risen life (Rom 6:3–4), Christians were no longer slaves to the baser instincts of their fallen human nature. The word had been sown and planted in their lives, producing the fruit of the Spirit (Gal 5:22–24). Paul showed pastor Titus how to shepherd his flock through the perils of temptation with Christ-centered virtue:

> For the grace of God has appeared, bringing salvation for all people, training us to renounce ungodliness and worldly passions, and to live self-controlled, upright, and godly lives in the present age, waiting for our blessed hope, the appearing of the glory of our great God and Savior Jesus Christ, who gave himself for us to redeem us from all lawlessness and to purify for himself a people for his own possession who are zealous for good works. (Titus 2:11–14)

The light of Christ continues to shine in this dark world, bringing hope to people held in bondage to sin and death. Christ Jesus equips his saints by sanctifying them by the bright beacon of his word of truth, guiding them safely through threats on every side.[33] That word led Christians in the ancient world to virtuous living, and it can do the same in our own morally turbulent world. We cannot turn the clock back to a simpler age, but we can be beacons of light and truth in a world that has lost its way morally and ethically.

Recapturing Virtue

The growing influence of expressive individualism leaves a sad moral legacy in its wake. Moral philosopher Alasdair MacIntyre traces a loss of the "language of morality" in the '70s and '80s.[34] Theologian David Wells observes that by the '90s we had become "morally obliterated"; people were not only "morally illiterate, but morally vacant."[35] By the dawn of the twenty-first century, sociologist James Davison Hunter noted America's near complete secularization: "Character is dead. Attempts to revive it will yield little. ... Social and cultural conditions that make character possible are no longer present and no amount of political rhetoric, legal maneuvering, educational policy making, or money can change that reality."[36]

The founders of America wanted to preserve the Christian consensus on public virtue while keeping church and state separate. By simultaneously prohibiting the establishment of religion and guaranteeing its free exercise in the Constitution's first amendment, they sought a cultural foundation for the new nation resting on the twin pillars of traditional virtue and religious conviction.[37] John Adams wrote, "Our Constitution was made only for a moral and religious people. It is wholly inadequate to the government of any other."[38]

But religious influence is rapidly vanishing. What should be done about morality in a secular age? In an effort to recapture cultural virtue, return to a moral society, reject secularism, and reclaim America's conservative constitutional vision, some church leaders advocate what they call "Christian nationalism."[39] They're distressed by watching the country they love descend into indulgent moral decay and have launched an activist political campaign to restore cultural virtue.

The Political Approach

Zealous authors sound the alarm, inciting Christians to step up and do their patriotic duty to retake American culture. They urge the American church to wake up, join a particular political party, mobilize, unite, and oust the progressive agenda through overt political action. In their view, failure to act is tantamount to sitting cowardly by while a new Nazi Germany emerges among us.[40] Such strident hyperbole divides the church.[41]

There's a more faithful approach for concerned citizens. Christians live *in* this world but not *of* it. The church doesn't seek to build God's kingdom through political action but to change hearts and lives by the power of the Holy Spirit working through the word. Christians are called to civic responsibility and love of neighbor wherever they live. On the one hand, God rules the world through political structures and authorities (Rom 13:1), but on the other hand, he governs the church by means of his word (Eph 2:19–22). Fostering a robust culture of the word protects against confusing these two forms of government or stressing political entities over our identity in Christ.

Two Kingdoms

Being of the *word* (and not of the *world*) means Christians see beyond this world's political structures. It allows them to see how God established two distinct kingdoms—the temporal and spiritual, working simultaneously for human good. In the temporal realm, God orders society using magistrates and rulers over citizens, parents over children, and pastors and elders over congregations. These are called the "three estates" as they give divinely created order to (1) the state, (2) the family, and (3) the church. In the spiritual realm, God rules directly over all believers, providing forgiveness, life, and salvation in Christ Jesus through the means of grace—his word and sacraments. His rule is not an oppressive hierarchy but an orderly system of benevolent care.

Order and reason are God's left-hand tools in the temporal kingdom. God's word and Holy Spirit are his right-hand tools in the spiritual kingdom. These two distinct kingdoms are unfortunately often confused. On the one extreme, people seek to promote the Christian faith, particularly Christian virtue, by political means instead of God's word working in people's hearts. On the other, government power is used to suppress free exercise of religion in public society. Being *of* the word yet *in* the world allows Christians to hold these two kingdoms in continual tension as they engage the complexities of living in any society. It allows neither withdrawal from civic duty nor the coercion of faith.

Jesus did not come into this world to establish a temporal kingdom but an eternal kingdom rooted in his word, wherein all humankind is made right with God to live together forever in a new heaven and new earth in glory everlasting.

In the world but not *of* it is the compelling vision that impels us forward in mission in this fallen world. The love of Christ urges us on (2 Cor 5:14). God has already reconciled the world unto himself through Jesus, not counting sinners' trespasses against them (5:19). So, we must forge bravely on. We do not represent ourselves but the one who died for all and rose again. We are ambassadors for Christ, entrusted with his message of reconciliation and building his spiritual kingdom.

The apostle Paul sometimes suffered abuse because he didn't use political pressure as his primary approach. Yet he didn't forfeit his rights as a Roman citizen (Acts 22:25), even appealing to Caesar for redress of wrongs (25:11). He called upon fellow Christians to be responsible citizens in a pagan culture while trusting in Christ Jesus as savior and Lord (Rom 13). Christians today are called to live in both of God's kingdoms, showing love for their Lord and love for their neighbor simultaneously. Being of the *word* rather than of the *world* requires constant vigilance, particularly when the world's political way to get things done appears easier, quicker, and more powerful.

A Kingdom Not of This World

No one particular political party or candidate can usher in the kingdom of God. God reminded ancient Israel what their ultimate allegiance should be: "Put not your trust in princes. ...

Blessed is he whose help is the God of Jacob, whose hope is in the LORD his God" (Ps 146:3, 5).

God's kingdom—though very much in the world—transcends all earthly powers. Jesus explained to the Roman governor Pontius Pilate that his kingdom posed no threat to Caesar's empire. "My kingdom is not of this world. If my kingdom were of this world, my servants would have been fighting, that I might not be delivered over to the Jews. But my kingdom is not from the world" (John 18:36).

Like Pilate, the disciples knew the impact of political power. They had been fixated on the restoration of the Davidic kingdom for a long time. They pined for the return of a divine monarchy, wherein the laws of the Torah would be enforced, Israelites would be in charge, and gentiles kept at bay in the outer temple courtyard. They didn't fully grasp how God ruled in this world by his word until after Pentecost.

The Power Struggle

Christians today struggle with the same issue: the allure of power. Amid the moral decay of the West, we often long for the restoration of our own version of a renewed Davidic kingdom: the restoration of Christendom with all its inherent privileges and advantages for Christians. Everything looks better in the rearview mirror. Christendom seems more appealing once it lies in ruin. Nostalgia takes over. The certainty of the past seems better than the distresses of the present or the unknowns of the future. We keep thinking we can bring back what we once had if we can just outsmart our opponents.

The social and ideological divides of our time trigger continual clashes over power and position. Cultural Marxism and neofascism (plus all their related ideologies) breed contempt and hatred, dividing humanity into various tribalist and racist categories of us versus them. Ever since Cain killed his own brother Abel after their parents' fall, bitter animosity has plagued humankind. The ensuing rancor intensifies when unfettered emotion takes the place of rational discourse and reasoned debate.

As society unravels and treasured institutions are deconstructed and dismantled in the resulting melee, many suffer from the delusion that these divides can be resolved politically, which brings about continual power struggles. If our preferred leaders were in charge, they reason, we could somehow impose better structures and wield power more effectively to put things back in proper order. But God's kingdom never comes by means of the ballot box.

Jesus's reminder that his kingdom is not of this world highlights the importance of what it means to be of the *word* rather than of the *world* and why cultivating the culture of the word in this perpetual political power grab is so vital. While facing Satan's temptations, Jesus cited the authority of the word of God (Matt 4:8–10). The allure of worldly power will always be part of Satan's tactics to tempt Christians away from the bright beacon of the word, so they eventually become *of* the world—despite their good intentions to the contrary. Our Lord shows us the way through these wilderness temptations.

Christ's kingdom grows today just as it did when the church was young. It comes by means of the word, as the word of God is sown, takes root, then grows in the hearts and lives of individuals to build up the body of Christ in every place on earth and under every form of political government.

A Spiritual Kingdom

To make political advancements the chief priority and purpose of the church guts her of her divinely given identity and purpose. She is not just one more partisan movement among many, according to Paul, but God's very own household, the "pillar and buttress of the truth" (1 Tim 3:15). To be sure, Christians may eagerly exercise civic duty, serve in political office, or even pursue legal redress, but ultimately their allegiance is elsewhere. Though the church seeks to be a light in society, working for equity and justice, peace and tranquility, decency and honor wherever she finds herself, she remains objective. Down through the ages she has lived under every possible political system or earthly government, including some led by godless villains. Wherever she lives in any country, free or oppressed, she prays for kings and all in authority to lead a peaceful and quiet life for the sake of the mission of "God our Savior, who desires all people to be saved and to come to the knowledge of the truth" (2:3–4).

In the end, our struggle as Christians is not really political but cosmic as we battle against the spiritual forces of wickedness in the heavenly realms (Eph 6:12). The church's confidence in this battle is rooted securely in the word of God and the continual prayer of her victorious Lord: "Sanctify them in the truth; your word is truth" (John 17:17). When Jesus prays that we would be sanctified, in effect he's pleading to the Father in heaven: *Cleanse them, guard them, keep them safe from this world's temptations and assaults*. In other words, *make them holy just as I am holy*. The Savior's fervent prayer is the church's abiding hope and confidence. It guides her way through various social upheavals in every troubled era, including ours.

Accountability and Reconciliation

Despite immense challenges all around us, Christians after Christendom are people of hope. We look not to the things that are seen but the things unseen (2 Cor 4:18). What is visible is temporary and fleeting. Only the word of the Lord lasts forever (1 Pet 1:25). That's why it stands at the center of the church's culture and why we sow it so diligently, especially during times of social unrest.

The word shows how the Lord held ancient Israel accountable for its systemic failure to remain faithful to him and care for the marginalized and oppressed, such as widows and orphans (Isa 1, 5). It shows why nations need to be called to account for failure to care for the downtrodden and subjugated.

The church therefore leads the way today, courageously repenting of its own prejudices and past failures and continually seeking to care for the oppressed and reconcile the divided.

The process is often messy and complicated, but it's what we are called to do. That's what happens when the word of God is planted, sprouts, and bears fruit. A culture of the word develops in word and deed, lives are changed, and hope awakens as eyes are focused on the cross of Christ.

What is set in motion here and now in Christ's church in the proclamation of his word and administration of his sacraments will come to fruition in the world yet to come, where saints from every nation, language, and ethnicity will be gathered around the throne of God in eternal victory. That glorious vision drives us ever onward in confident mission.

Eyes Ahead

Unfortunately, we have a tendency to look backward. We long for the past, hoping somehow to resurrect what once was but is no more. That would be a poor application of history and a still worse application of the Bible. God's word teaches us to look to the past with both repentance and thanksgiving: repentance for our collective and personal sins and thanksgiving for God's grace and mercy so abundantly evident in every generation, providing confident hope for the future.

In the world but ever *of* the word. Through the centuries, that's how the church has lived in mission. This is the culture of the word in motion. This approach works just as well in our turbulent times as it did in the apostolic era. Clear-eyed, we are not deterred by threats on every side. Ours is not a ministry to the culture but to blood-bought souls who have lost their way.

To the burdened and the broken we bring enduring hope and abundant life. It is the hope and life of Christ Jesus, rooted in the transcendent power of his word and the culture it produces. With our feet planted squarely in this present world, we draw life from the world to come in order to bring new life to people in this world who have lost their identity and purpose.

We have our eyes on the ultimate prize. We look ahead to this world's final chapter and the culmination of our salvation, "waiting for our blessed hope, the appearing of the glory of our great God and Savior Jesus Christ, who gave himself for us to redeem us from all lawlessness and to purify for himself a people for his own possession who are zealous for good works" (Titus 2:13–14). Christ Jesus, the Lamb of God who takes away the sins of the world, will one day shepherd all the faithful in eternal glory. There they will see with their own risen eyes what they now behold only dimly by faith.

Long ago, in a time of cultural chaos and collapse very much like our own, Bishop Aurelius Augustine stressed the significance of this new creation for Christians under fire daily:

> There is no need here to speak in detail of each of these seven "days." Suffice it to say that this "seventh day" will be our Sabbath and that it will end in no evening, but only in the Lord's day—that eighth and eternal day

> which dawned when Christ's resurrection heralded an eternal rest both for the spirit and for the body. On that day we shall rest and see, see and love, love and praise—for this is to be the end without the end of all our living, that Kingdom without end, the real goal of our present life.[42]

In the tempestuous winds of these times our hearts remain firmly fixed on the timeless joys ahead. It is our privilege to sow the word of truth and grow a culture of the word tailored for this present cultural moment. Our final chapter offers some practical considerations on how to do this. As the word is sown, its culture is grown.

CHAPTER 6

The Church Grows from the Culture of the Word

When they had preached the gospel to that city [Derbe] and had made many disciples, they returned to Lystra and to Iconium and to Antioch, strengthening the souls of the disciples, encouraging them to continue in the faith, and saying that through many tribulations we must enter the kingdom of God. And when they had appointed elders for them in every church, with prayer and fasting they committed them to the Lord in whom they had believed.

Acts 14:21–23

It's time we depart and prayerfully commit you to the Lord. But like the apostles long ago in Asia Minor, first we want to strengthen your souls and encourage you to continue in the faith with some practical considerations.

Like the New Testament disciples, you will encounter many tribulations along the way. But don't lose heart. The Lord is faithful and will see his church through to the end. The gates of hell will not prevail (Matt 16:18). Of course, that's not permission to become complacent. The declining church of the West should make that abundantly clear. Rather it's a call to stalwart faithfulness balanced by vigorous zeal to "seek and save the lost" (Luke 19:10), which is precisely the result when the culture of the word takes root and grows.

As we've stressed, wherever the seed is sown, the culture is grown. That's the word of God at work. The New Testament church testifies again and again to the power of God's word. But there's no magic formula for mission in an antagonistic world. In fact, it can be time-consuming and hard work, and we may not see the results of our labor.

To faithfully grow the culture of the word there were four areas of good soil the New Testament church chose as places in which to sow the word: worship, catechesis, hospitality, and vocation. These areas remain vital to the church and must be engaged to ensure the seed is sown robustly.

Correspondingly, we want to highlight three skills the church cultivated to grow this culture of the word: commonsense contextualization, holy discernment, and adaptive capacity. Our sending word of encouragement highlights these areas and skills to underscore how the word can best be sown and its culture grown in our own day.

Worship

To cultivate the word in our neopagan society, worship remains central, as it has since the church's beginning. This is the throbbing heart of mission throughout history. There the Word of God is sown in speech and song, and thus its culture grows from age to age and place to place. We worship a radically different God than the god of this age (2 Cor 4:4). Our glorious Lord Jesus Christ continually grows a kingdom for himself through his word. He gathers a holy assembly and communion by means of his transforming and transcendent word. In the public preaching of God's holy word and communion around the Lord's table, the Holy Spirit calls, gathers, and enlightens a holy people with his gifts of forgiveness, life, and salvation.

This gathered church sings the eternal song of the Lord in earthly accents. Her musicians use instruments and sounds indigenous to their own cultures to extol God the Father through his son Jesus Christ in the power and presence of the Holy Spirit. Christians do not come together to be amused or entertained. They come for an earthly audience with their heavenly Lord; Jesus himself is present in his word and meal. Worship is heaven on earth; worshipers gather to meet God himself. In his holy presence there is light and peace even in a dark, distressing world.

Tunes modern and ancient are woven together. Harmony, rhythm, and tonality vary with the time and place, but the theme of that transcendent song fixes hearts and minds on one thing: "the appearing of the glory of *our great God and Savior Jesus Christ*" (Titus 2:13, emphasis added).

Word-centered worship may be many things, but it's never dull or boring. God condescends to dwell among his people by means of his word, just as he did in Israel's tabernacle and temple, inviting them to come into his presence to find their joy and rest in him. And so anxious hearts are brave again and arms are strong to serve. In worship centered on Christ and rooted in his word, Jesus himself is pleased to dwell with us just as he did in apostolic times: "Let the word of Christ dwell in you richly, teaching and admonishing one another in all wisdom, singing psalms and hymns and spiritual songs, with thankfulness in your hearts to God" (Col 3:16).

In transcultural and transcendent worship there is life and light in a world of darkness and death. Word-centered worship is enlivened by the invisible presence of the Word made flesh, Christ Jesus our Lord. In his flesh and by his blood there is full and free remission from all sin: Guilt is erased, shame removed, and honor bestowed over and over again until the end of time.

Word-Focused Worship

1. Is worship in your congregation focused on God or the worshipers? Which markers indicate its focus?

2. How does your usual order of worship indicate the word of God, prayer, and the Lord's Supper are central? How do your hymns and songs teach and inculcate the word in the hearts and lives of worshipers?

3. How can technology support rather than displace embodied fellowship in your congregation?

4. In a culture where few people sing, how will you teach your congregation to sing together easily and confidently?

5. Who are the people you need to facilitate and enhance the public worship services of your church (ushers, greeters, musicians, etc.)? How will you recruit and train them?

Catechesis

Catechesis and preaching are united in the church's life and mission. The church preaches what she teaches, teaches what she preaches, and then lives it out (Luke 11:28). The seed is the word of God. That seed grows its own unique culture among believing Christians. The power to produce the fruits of faith lies not in the preacher or the teacher but in the word that is preached and taught (8:11). In a rapidly shifting social context, the church keeps announcing and reannouncing the living word of the living Christ to a dying world.

Catechesis is the faithful teaching of God's word to each new generation. The church's catechesis sows the transcendent and transforming word deep into the hearts and lives of young and old—newly committed believers and life-long Christians alike. Catechesis begins with the core texts of the faith: the Ten Commandments, the Apostles' Creed, and the Lord's Prayer.[43] When people learn these foundational texts by heart, committing them to memory by rehearsing them orally and using them faithfully, they learn how to build their lives and prayers around them. The word of God then increasingly takes root and grows, just as it did in the apostolic church.

Faithful catechesis spans cultures and time. Moses captured the Lord's instruction for how it was first done among the Israelites:

> And these words that I command you today shall be on your heart. You shall teach them diligently to your children, and shall talk of them when you sit in your house, and when you walk by the way, and when you lie down, and when you rise. You shall bind them as a sign on your hand, and they shall be as frontlets between your eyes. You shall write them on the doorposts of your house and on your gates. (Deut 6:6–9)

Paul urged Timothy toward faithful catechesis: "the pattern of sound words" (2 Tim 1:13). Later, the early church developed simplified creeds to teach, uphold, and defend the faith, particularly during times of controversy. During the Reformation, pastors and Reformers formalized catechesis by putting the chief teachings of Scripture into simplified instruction books called catechisms. In that time of biblical illiteracy, they were tools to pass on the faith in households while providing a common language and understanding in congregations. The core scriptural texts of the Ten Commandments, the Apostles' Creed, and the Lord's Prayer shaped Christian morality and spirituality from one generation to the next.

Catechisms remain a profound tool today for the young and old to inwardly digest the key texts of Scripture, informing and forming who they are and what they do as disciples of Christ. They provide a template for the church to sow the word in succeeding generations: to "teach [it] diligently to your children, and talk of [it] when you sit in your house, and when you walk by the way, and when you lie down, and when you rise" (Deut 6:7). Thus, one generation tells the next the joyous good news of how God saved the whole world in his son Christ Jesus.

> O God, from my youth you have taught me,
> and I still proclaim your wondrous deeds.
> So even to old age and gray hairs,
> O God, do not forsake me,
> until I proclaim your might to another generation,
> your power to all those to come. (Ps 71:17–18)

Where God's word is patiently sown through consistent, faithful catechesis and takes root, the culture of the word grows and flourishes from one generation to another until the end of time.

Word-Focused Catechesis

1. How can your congregation develop better and more effective catechesis in every household (Deut 6:6–7)?
2. How will your congregation and its workers formally and informally catechize new members in the central texts of the faith (Ps 119:11)?
3. How will you integrate life-long catechesis into your congregation's rhythms so that everyone continues to grow in the knowledge of the breadth, length, height, and depth of God's love in Christ Jesus (Eph 3:17–19)?

Vocation

Jesus taught Christians to serve him by serving others. He hides himself in our neighbors' needs. When we clothe the naked, feed the hungry, welcome the stranger, or visit the sick and imprisoned, we are actually serving him. "Truly, I say to you, as you did it to one of the least of these my brothers, you did it to me" (Matt 25:40).

Likewise, God accomplishes his divine works on earth through various earthly callings in three estates: home, state, and church. These callings are not merely jobs or occupations, but each is a God-given *vocation* or office for various stations in life. Through these distinct offices God himself tends to the needs of all humanity in body and soul. He raises children from infancy to adulthood through fathers and mothers. He provides for public safety and welfare through governing officials and institutions. Jesus uses his church to proclaim his word, forgiving penitent sinners—first calling, then gathering and ultimately sanctifying them by his Spirit (John 20:21–23). Those who are catechized by the word and worship according to the word live out their vocations according to that word.

Family

Marriage and the family are not social constructs. Their origin can be traced back to God's creation of Eve from Adam and God's efficacious benediction: "Be fruitful and multiply and fill the earth and subdue it" (Gen 1:28). Ever since, God has given husbands to wives and wives to husbands and children to parents and parents to children, lavishing on them his care and blessing as they serve one another in love (Eph 6:1–4). The word gives order to the family and shapes the most intimate part of our lives to be lived freely and confidently according to that word. Human identity is shaped at the start, beginning in the family. A culture of the word upholds the family, celebrates the family, and defends the family.

State

Though governing institutions may be viewed politically or historically, essentially they are God's instruments to establish justice, ensure domestic tranquility, provide for a common defense, and promote the general welfare of the populace of every nation: "There is no authority except from God, and those that exist have been instituted by God" (Rom 13:1). Although God has instituted government for the good of humankind, not every government is inherently godly in action or behavior. When it veers toward evil, the vocation of Christian citizenship requires that we obey God and his word rather than wicked or tyrannical authorities, despite any consequences we may have to endure. We are called to use available methods of redress and fitting action to speak for the marginalized and oppressed as we call for justice and virtuous change. The estate of government and our vocation of citizenship go hand in hand and are guided by God's word.

Church

Though churches may seem to be human organizations sharing a common interest between leaders and followers just like other earthly associations, they are actually spiritual fellowships of souls knit together by their shared faith in one Lord, Jesus Christ: "I will build my church and the gates of hell will not prevail against it" (Matt 16:18b). Pastors are emissaries of the heavenly bridegroom who tends his earthly bride by his word and meal (Eph 4:11–13). Believers are royal priests who serve God in everything they do and say (1 Pet 2:9).

The church cultivates a sense of divine vocation in this chaotic world, confident that God's word will prosper in the purpose for which he sent it, yielding a rich and abundant harvest in terms of outward stability and internal peace (Isa 55:11).

Word-Focused Vocation

1. How can your congregation equip members to publicly honor and support marriage and the family, strengthening husbands and wives, parents and children in their God-given vocations (Eph 6:1–4)?

2. How will your congregation inspire members to use their professional training, business expertise, and daily vocations to serve the common good in local society (1 Tim 2:1–3)?

3. How can your congregation encourage members to be informed and active citizens locally and nationally, exercising their civic duties for the common good, while prioritizing membership in Christ's kingdom above all else (Matt 22:21)?

4. Which resources might your congregation use to establish a biblical framework for an objective and dispassionate discussion of popular destructive cultural trends and ideologies (Col 4:6)?

5. How will your congregation cooperate with community officials and programs to serve the common good and defend the vulnerable, without compromising its distinctly Christian integrity and purpose (1 Pet 2:13–17)?
6. How can your congregation train and equip your members to model and display kindness and civility in rational discourse as they actively exercise their civic rights in the public sphere (1 Pet 3:8–9)?

Hospitality

The church is an embodied community. When Christians cannot see and touch those with whom they are united in faith, genuine fellowship suffers. Sharing one another's burdens and joys is one of the distinguishing marks of Christian love. It's the way we fulfill the law of Christ, who commanded us to love one another just as he has loved us (Gal 6:2; John 13:34). In such caring interchanges, sorrows are divided and joys are multiplied. Remote connections will not suffice. The care of souls among Christians is supported and enhanced by real, physical interactions with one another.

Early Christians stood out in a fractured and contentious society by the genuine love they expressed to everyone but, especially, to their fellow Christians (Gal 6:10). Likewise, today, in a world full of lonely and burdened people, hospitality toward unbelievers is likely the single most remarkable thing we can do in support of the Christian mission. It was an essential obligation for early Christians: "Do not neglect to show hospitality to strangers, for thereby some have entertained angels unawares" (Heb 13:2); "Show hospitality to one another without grumbling" (1 Pet 4:9). Paul even lists hospitality among the qualifying traits for pastors (1 Tim 3:2).

Hospitality begins at home. The remarkable generosity of opening one's house to others is valued across cultures. When people sit together over a common meal, they share meaningful conversations. Often in this relaxed context the seed of the word of God can be first planted, and then nurtured, eventually maturing into the harvest of a living faith. The lowly dining table can make a significant difference for time and eternity when the culture of the word takes root and grows there as family members and guests alike are evangelized and catechized by God's living word.

Face to face with others at church—as well as around the table in our homes—the word of God is sown and its culture grows. Souls are cared for, fed, and nurtured. That's why hospitality is always part of mission, just as it was among the first Christians in Jerusalem:

> And day by day, attending the temple together and breaking bread in their homes, they received their food with glad and generous hearts, praising God and having favor with all people. (Acts 2:46–47)

Word-Focused Hospitality

1. How can you identify the talents and skills of people of all ages in your congregation (1 Cor 12:12–20)?

2. How will you encourage these people to use their abilities to build an environment of hospitality among your church?

3. How will your congregation express meaningful hospitality toward those who visit its public worship?

4. How can your congregation meaningfully engage the various ethnicities and marginal groups in its community, remaining attentive to everyone's need for spiritual care and healing?

5. What practical tools for personal and family word-centered prayer can you develop for households of all ages to use around their tables?

6. How can your congregation assist members to routinely schedule and honor family mealtime, and then extend personal hospitality toward the lonely, outcast, and alienated in their neighborhoods and social circles?

These four areas—worship, catechesis, vocation, and hospitality—have nurtured the culture of the word throughout the church's history. They are the good soil into which the word is to be sown again and again (Matt 13:23).

Skills for Mission after Christendom

Besides these four central areas where the word is sown, there are three corresponding skills that help the local congregation grow the culture of the word. They are especially pertinent for the congregation's organizational aspects, enhancing its ability to grow the culture of the word and its unchanging truth amid a changing landscape. Those skills are: commonsense contextualization, holy discernment, and adaptive capacity. In a setting that increasingly resembles the paganized secular environment of the early Christians, we need to remain skilled in these areas just as the church across the ages was.

Commonsense Contextualization

Commonsense contextualization grows nimble missionaries. Christians must always "test the spirits" against the word of God when it comes to doctrine and practice (1 John 4:1–3). Common sense determines faithful contextualization, as we noted in chapter 2 of this book. Human audiences with varied customs and expectations call for different approaches when it comes to sowing the seed of the word of God. Likewise, shifting cultural expectations have an impact on how the unchanging truths of his word are preached and taught over time.

Yet cultural context should never eclipse the text of God's word. Text always takes priority over context. Christians are called to be discerning in terms of cultural fads and trends. Which current ideas can be adapted or reformed to serve the teaching of the word? Which ones must be rejected or actively resisted as antithetical to it?

What happens if political pressure removes local churches' real estate tax exemptions and they are no longer able to own and maintain dedicated church buildings? What happens if full-time clergy salaries and benefits become an unaffordable luxury? Holy discernment, commonsense contextualization, and adaptive capacity will be essential then.

Luxurious buildings and well-paid clergy have not been the norm throughout Christian history; we can learn that from reading the book of Acts. Yet, the word is sown and grows today the same way it did in the apostolic era when it produced the culture of the word. That first congregation in Jerusalem "devoted themselves to the apostles' teaching" (Acts 2:42)—that is, the word of God proclaimed by Christ's authorized representatives. Preaching by trained and qualified ministers remains essential no matter how circumstances change. "Faith comes from hearing," after all, "and hearing through the word of Christ" (Rom 10:17). The culture feeds on change, but the church feeds on God's unchanging word (Matt 24:35).

From the Father through the Son in the Holy Spirit, then back again in the Spirit through the Son to the Father, everything we have comes from God and everything we do flows back to him in a perpetual divine cycle (Col 3:15–17). This is God's wheel that moves the church into hearts and lives across the world. His word accomplishes the mission by his power, not ours (Mark 4:26–28). His word is sown, takes root, then grows into an abundance. Believing men and women bear witness to that word in their daily vocations, and the Lord continues to add others to their number (Acts 2:47).

Holy Discernment

Every passing ideology and cultural trend requires discernment and sanctified common sense. Christians must accurately examine and assess each one in light of the word of God. Where cultural shifts are in clear violation of the express will of God revealed in his word, or where they conflict with the law of love for Jesus's sake, the church must pursue a course of active *resistance*. Where she has willfully or mistakenly adopted destructive patterns of thought and behavior, she will *repent*. Where she is able to harness and adapt cultural trends in service of the culture of the word, she will gladly *receive* and *reform* them for the glory of God and the benefit of her neighbors.

These four responses—resistance, repentance, reception, and reform—provide a faithful posture toward the world in which the Lord of the church has placed us as his emissaries.[44] Holy discernment allows the church to cultivate her culture so the word can grow without infestation from the weeds of this present ungodly age or a rigid fixation on the modalities of the past.

The church's task is to make skillful use of wisdom according to God's word—holy discernment, in other words—as she supports the culture of the word in her administrative forms and structures. Examples of this are replete in the Scriptures, even in pagan contexts.

> Then the king commanded Ashpenaz, his chief eunuch, to bring some of the people of Israel, both of the royal family and of the nobility, youths without blemish, of good appearance and skillful in all wisdom, endowed with knowledge, understanding learning, and competent to stand in the king's palace, and to teach them the literature and language of the Chaldeans. (Dan 1:3–4)

Daniel, Shadrach, Meshach, and Abednego were selected. As their story unfolds, we see how they were able to use holy discernment, to be "skillful in all wisdom," during their time of change and unrest while exiled in their new pagan environment. They also demonstrated the use of commonsense contextualization by assuming pagan names. Yet they refused to compromise the word of God or the life God had called them to live. In other words, though they encountered tribulation and trial, they trusted the word to lead the way. Paul did the same when standing trial before the governing authorities (Acts 26:19–23). Early Christians had to regularly discern how they would respond to the culture even as the pagan gentiles were being welcomed in (15:6–21).

In our time, we ought to do the same. We're not called to repristinate the heady days of the apostolic era, the heroic struggles of the Middle Ages, or the comparatively comfortable role the church played in postwar America in the middle of the last century. Reinstating preferred models or a return to the past is not a reasonable response to a shifting culture. The church is not handicapped by change, needing to recover what she used to have in days gone by. She moves ever forward, strengthened by each new challenging generation with confidence and hope, rooted and grounded in the unchanging word of God.

We are called to be beacons of hope in the present, bright with promise, though uncertainty often clouds our illumination. Complex matters deserve our full attention. Holy discernment clings to the truth of God's word and abides by the fruit of the Spirit as seen in the virtues, particularly the exercise of holy wisdom.

Adaptive Capacity

Throughout its history, the church has devised institutions to facilitate effective sowing of the word. She has shown an immense capacity to adapt to shifting cultural circumstances. Diaconal ministry was introduced in Jerusalem to safeguard the equitable distribution of aid for widows in the first Christian congregation (Acts 6:1–3). Yet the apostles took great care to ensure that word-rooted mission remained the heart and center of their life together: "But we will devote ourselves to prayer and to the ministry of the word" (Acts 6:4).

That's been the challenge down through the centuries. By their very nature, church institutions need continual evaluation and redirection. The church needs to uphold good order and maintain a functional structure, but secondary matters all too easily take precedence over primary matters. Essential things languish and wither, while secondary things become enshrined in institutionalized bureaucracy.

In our chaotic and rapidly shifting culture, the church must be especially agile, critiquing and reevaluating its structures in view of new and unprecedented circumstances. Church constitutions and bylaws developed thirty or fifty years ago rarely enable nimble ministry today. The natural inclination toward institutionalism for institutionalism's sake must be actively resisted.

Congregations and church bodies alike should regularly review their organizational structures, lest their outdated governance models foster the idolatrous view that the church is a legal entity rather than the divinely instituted body of Christ. As cultural influences morph and shift, continual adaptive capacity skills become increasingly important.

To be responsive to our shifting cultural environment and yet continue on faithfully, we need to polish our skills in commonsense contextualization, holy discernment, and adaptive capacity.

Enhancing Contextualization Skills

1. Regularly conduct a demographic study of your surrounding community, augmented by public focus groups, to gain an accurate picture of the socioeconomic makeup of your community, as well as its values, priorities, and commonly held ideologies.

2. Develop a strategic plan for your congregation to cultivate a public witness faithful to the text of God's word in your present cultural context, using or repurposing your property to best serve that witness.

3. Devise a contingency plan for how your congregation will secure and/or support trained and qualified ministers should your finances dwindle.

Enhancing Holy Discernment Skills

1. Organize a discussion for pastors and church leaders about how to cultivate wisdom and think critically in an age that undercuts truth and logic.

2. Teach the young and old in your congregation how to use holy discernment in their daily vocations by implementing the four responses of resistance, repentance, reception, and reform.

Enhancing Adaptive Capacity Skills

1. Evaluate congregation governance structures as part of a regular strategic plan review: How do they support or impede the centrality of Christ and his cross-centered mission in your church?
2. Explore which avenues are open to your congregation to influence careful review and adjustment of procedures and bureaucracies in your church's affiliated denomination.

Beyond Survival

Some see the downfall of Christendom, the rise of secularism, and the resurgence of paganism as the death knell of the church. Those whose hope is in the Word made flesh know differently. Christians are undeterred by cultural disarray. We remain optimistic about the future. We're not idealists but realists. Yet, we take our reality seriously. Yes, there are formidable cultural forces lined up against much that we believe and hold dear, but we do not stand defenseless.

Opportunities hide behind the obstacles surrounding us on every side. We may never have faced these hurdles personally, but our ancestors in the faith did long before us. More than that, we know the one in whom we have believed can lead us safely through this present distress to the glories that await us (2 Tim 1:12). Our quiet hope in that future victory brings confident courage for current life and mission in Jesus's name.

Mission after Christendom is not a nostalgic effort to recover some hypothetical world that used to be but a rigorous and compassionate sowing of the word in the world of hurt we live in right now. We must focus on worship, catechesis, vocation, and hospitality just like our spiritual ancestors, while honing the skills they used: commonsense contextualization, holy discernment, and adaptive capacity.

We cannot keep on doing the same old thing, blithely ignoring reality and hoping for the best. The word and sacraments are not magic talismans designed only for us and people like us. We need to get out of our comfort zones and into our communities to sow the word where it can take root and grow in the hearts and lives of countless people who have lost their way. God the Father longs to welcome home his beloved daughters and sons. They will find asylum, rest, and healing in Christ's body, the church, as they await that final triumph.

Eyes on the Prize

The missional task has been daunting in every era. This book is our encouragement to God's people not to cave in the face of opposition but—like the early Christians in a pre-Christian society—to confidently press on to what ultimately lies ahead. We persist in following God's word even in a post-Christian society. The effort is well worth it. Though now we sow in tears, ultimately, we shall reap in joy (Matt 25:23; Ps 126:5). Where the word is sown the culture is grown.

The church is not a mere organization or human institution, but a living organism rooted and grounded in the word of God. You can't make it grow by your creative ingenuity and concerted effort. It's not up to you. The word of God always does what it says. We sow the seed, but God makes it grow. You can plant and you can water, but only God gives the increase (1 Cor 3:6). The kingdom of God comes all by itself through the power of the word; we pray that it may come among us as God sends forth his Spirit to make his word sprout and grow.

The Way of the Cross

Faithful followers of Jesus are prepared for struggle. "If anyone would come after me," he said, "let him deny himself and take up his cross and follow me. For whoever would save his life will lose it, but whoever loses his life for my sake will find it" (Matt 16:24–25). That can feel lonely at times. One can even get despondent, like Elijah, who felt he was the only one left speaking for the Lord. Tribulation will come. But we are certainly not left alone. The Lord reminded Elijah, "I will leave seven thousand in Israel, all the knees that have not bowed to Baal" (1 Kgs 19:18). On his cross Jesus endured complete abandonment in our place, and he calls us to bear his cross as a sign of his risen presence with us.

The Christian path is always marked by a cross. Humankind's way leads through life to death, but God's way leads through death to life. That's a hard lesson to learn, especially for eager overachievers like us. We keep thinking we should be able to make things happen if we work smart enough and hard enough and long enough. But this is not the way of the cross. We have to be prepared to let go of control and see where God leads by means of his word. The path of Jesus leads through suffering and death to resurrection and victory. "Truly, truly, I say to you," he reminds us, "unless a grain of wheat falls into the earth and dies, it remains alone; but if it dies, it bears much fruit" (John 12:24).

The seven churches of Asia Minor provide perspective on the lifespan of local congregations (Rev 2:1–3:22). Some were more faithful than others; all faced great challenges—even persecution—in the pagan world before Christendom. They all grew. Some thrived. But only one, Smyrna, exists today. That's a frequent pattern. Churches have a natural life cycle. Congregations come and go. Some grow impressively, only to shrivel and ultimately die. But Christ Jesus continues to preserve his beloved saints and establish them in his word. He equips the saints for service in his name after Christendom just as he did in previous generations. Those who serve the Lord Jesus are playing the long game. Ultimately, he will gather his church around his throne in glory. The final outcome is assured: "I am with you always, to the end of the age" (Matt 28:20).

To the End of the Earth

The Lord Jesus commissioned his apostles to take his gospel into all the world. "You will receive power when the Holy Spirit has come upon you, and you will be my witnesses in Jerusalem and in all Judea and Samaria, and to the end of the earth" (Acts 1:8). The book of Acts tells the story of how they sowed the seed of God's word throughout the ancient Mediterranean world, beginning in Jerusalem. Encountering a myriad of languages, cultures, and people groups, they gathered Jews and gentiles alike into one transcendent community of faith. In that thrilling story we find a template for mission that applies still today: where God's word is sown, its culture is grown.

In some places God's word was rejected and the apostles barely escaped with their lives (Acts 9:22–25; 14:5–7). In other places, it was met with joy and affirmation (Acts 10:44–48; 11:1–18). Yet in every place the word of the Lord grew, accomplishing the purpose for which he sent it (Isa 55:11).

The last chapter of Acts is the place to start looking at mission today. At the end of Paul's many missionary journeys, he was taken into custody and transported to far-off Rome for trial. According to oral history, there his enemies ultimately triumphed, and he was martyred. There's a lesson there for us. Though his mission was marked by a cross, at the end of his ministry Paul still welcomed all who came to him, "proclaiming the kingdom of God and teaching about the Lord Jesus Christ with all boldness and without hindrance" (Acts 28:31).

God's mission is generational and transcendent. Each generation tells the gospel to the next, right up to the end, when Christ returns to claim his own. And the gospel creates its own transcendent culture that welcomes believers from diverse lands, tribes, and customs into one transcultural communion extending through time and into eternity—to that bright new creation where time has ended, where death has died, and the kingdom of this world has become the kingdom of our Lord and of his Christ (Rev 11:15). In the meantime, we keep working: sowing the seed and growing the culture of the word to the glory of God and the salvation of many. Where the word is sown the culture is grown.

Now to him who is able to do far more abundantly
than all that we ask or think, according to the power
at work within us, to him be glory
in the church and in Christ Jesus
throughout all generations,
forever and ever. Amen.

Ephesians 3:20–21

Notes

1. In 2017 a Columbian threesome was given legal recognition as a family unit. Dimitri O'Donnell, "Meet Colombia's First Legally Recognized 'Throuple,' " NBC News, July 22, 2017, https://www.nbcnews.com/feature/nbc-out/meet-colombia-s-first-legally-recognized-throuple-n785541.
2. Anthony Esolen, "Mission Nary Impossible: The Unevangelized May Be Better and Worse than Savages," *Touchstone* 28, no. 1 (Jan/Feb 2015).
3. Charles Taylor, *A Secular Age* (Belknap Press, 2007).
4. Ross Douthat, "The Return to Paganism," *New York Times,* December 12, 2018.
5. See Steven D. Smith, *Pagans and Christians in the City* (Eerdmans, 2018); see also Anthony T. Kronman, *Confessions of a Born-Again Pagan* (Yale University Press, 2016).
6. For a snapshot of the Bible's dynamic power, see John W. Kleinig's provocative little book about God's big book, *God's Word: A Guide to Holy Scripture* (Lexham, 2022).
7. For an overview of the use and abuse of Matthew 28:20 as a mission paradigm, see Lucas Woodford, *Great*

Commission, Great Confusion, or Great Confession? The Mission of the Holy Christian Church (Wipf & Stock, 2012).

8. For the power of God's spoken and sacramental word in a dying world, see Harold Senkbeil, *Dying to Live: The Foundation, Focus, and Shape of the Christian Life*, 2nd ed. (Concordia, 2025).

9. Kevin Vanhoozer, *Hearers and Doers: A Pastor's Guide to Making Disciples through Scripture and Doctrine* (Lexham, 2019), 116–17, citing John Calvin's *Institutes of the Christian Religion* 1.6.1.

10. C. S. Lewis, *The Screwtape Letters* (HarperCollins, 1996), Letter 2.

11. Charlemagne was crowned emperor by Leo III on December 25, 800 in the old St. Peter's Basilica in Rome.

12. H. Richard Niebuhr, *Christ and Culture* (Harper & Row, 1951), 32.

13. For an examination of these movements, see Woodford, *Great Commission*.

14. Sean Benesh, *Metrospiritual: The Geography of Church Planting* (Resource Publishing, 2011).

15. Will Mancini and Cory Hartman, *Future Church: Seven Laws of Real Church Growth* (Baker Books, 2020).

16. Nicene Creed, ca. 451. See Phillip Cary, *The Nicene Creed: An Introduction* (Lexham, 2023), 7.

17. Nicene Creed.

18. Martin Luther, *Martin Luther's Christmas Book*, ed. Roland H. Bainton (Fortress Press, 1948), 22, 23.

19. See Harold Senkbeil, "Intentional Treatment," in *The Care of Souls* (Lexham, 2019), 99.

20. See Sean McGever, *Evangelism: For the Care of Souls* (Lexham, 2023), esp. chapter 5 on the changing cultural context of evangelism.

21. Notable apologetic works have surfaced in recent decades. Foremost are the works of Lee Strobel and Tim Keller: Strobel, *The Case for Faith* (Zondervan, 2000); Keller, *The Reason for God: Belief in an Age of Skepticism* (Penguin Books, 2009). However, they assume the cultural tolerance and acceptance of Christianity from an earlier era.

22. Aaron Renn has identified markers for this change. The peak apologetic days were seen in what he calls the neutral era (1994–2014); Aaron Renn, *Life in the Negative World: Confronting Challenges in an Anti-Christian Culture* (Zondervan, 2024), 6–7.

23. See Nicholas Carr, *The Shallows: What the Internet Is Doing to Our Brains* (W. W. Norton, 2011), and Sherry Turkle, *Alone Together: Why We Expect More from Technology and Less from Each Other* (Basic Books, 2012). See also the documentary *Childhood 2.0* (2020) that explores growing up in the age of social media and its impact on human development.

24. See Senkbeil, *The Care of Souls,* for an overview of the classic art of the pastoral care of souls.

25. As of 2023, 70% of churches have 100 or less in attendance weekly; only 10% have more than 250; Jim Davis and Michael Graham, *The Great Dechurching* (Zondervan, 2023), 12.

26. See Phillip Magness, *Church Music: For the Care of Souls* (Lexham, 2023); Keith and Kristyn Getty, *Sing! How Worship Transforms Your Life, Family, and Church* (B&H Books, 2017); Paul Westermeyer, *Te Deum: The Church and Music* (Fortress Press, 1998).

27. Thomas Winger, "Liturgy: Lutheran Confessional Theology, Presuppositions, and Definitions," in *LSB Companion to the Services* (CPH, 2022), 15.

28. Although Rod Dreher in *The Benedict Option: A Strategy for Christians in a Post-Christian Nation* (Sentinel Publishing, 2017) explores faithful mission in an antagonistic culture, overall it seems to reinforce an isolationist stance.

29. Robert Jenson, "It's the Culture: How the West Became Deaf to the Biblical Voice That Had Led It," *First Things,* no. 243 (2014): 33–36.

30. Nancy Pearcey's book, *Love Thy Body: Answering Hard Questions about Life and Sexuality* (Baker Books, 2018), is extremely helpful in unpacking this issue.

31. Abigail Shrier discusses this malady at length in *Irreversible Damage: The Transgender Craze Seducing Our Daughters* (Regnery Publishing, 2021).

32. Aristotle, *The Nicomachean Ethics* (Penguin Classics, 2004).

33. C. Kavin Rowe observes that Christianity does not offer instant solutions to society's predicaments or "somehow return us to a more 'Christian' culture. The surprise is rather that Christians can bring good news in the midst of a vastly complicated world and live in ways that give us hope in the face of demise and death." *Christianity's Surprise: A Sure and Certain Hope* (Abingdon Press, 2020), 95.

34. Alasdair MacIntyre, *After Virtue,* 2nd ed. (Notre Dame Press, 2002), 2.

35. David Wells, *Losing Our Virtue: Why the Church Must Recover Its Moral Vision* (Eerdmans, 1998), 13.

36. James Davison Hunter, *The Death of Character: Moral Education in an Age Without Good or Evil* (Basic Books, 2001), xii.

37. Their plan was to balance freedom and morality. Freedom without morality is anarchy. Morality without freedom is theocracy. The Constitution established a grand framework of checks and balances in the three branches of government.

38. "From John Adams to the Massachusetts Militia, 11 October, 1798," National Archives, https://founders.archives.gov/documents/Adams/99-02-02-3102.

39. See Stephen Wolfe, *The Case for Christian Nationalism* (Cannon Press, 2022).

40. See Eric Metaxas, *Letter to the American Church* (Salem Books, 2022).

41. Balanced appraisals of the Christian Nationalism movement include Tim Perry, *When Politics Becomes Heresy: The Idol of Power and the Gospel of Christ* (Lexham Press, 2025), and Neil Shenvi's comprehensive review of Wolfe's book, "Of God's and Men: A Long Review of Wolfe's Case for Christian Nationalism," Neil Shenvi—Apologetics, https://shenviapologetics.com/of-gods-and-men-a-long-review-of-wolfes-case-for-christian-nationalism-part-i-book-summary/. More critical assessments can be found in Tim Alberta, *The Kingdom, the Power, and the Glory: American Evangelicals in an Age of Extremism* (Harper, 2023); and Philip Gorski and Samuel Perry, *The Flag and the Cross: White Christian Nationalism and the Threat to American Democracy* (Oxford University Press, 2022).

42. Augustine of Hippo, *The City of God: Books XVII–XXII*, ed. H. Dressler, trans. G. G. Walsh and D. J. Honan (Catholic University of America Press, 1954), 24:510–11.

43. For guidance on how to incorporate these texts into daily life and prayer use your denominational catechetical tools, or see Peter Leithart, Ben Myers, and Wesley Hill, *The Collected Christian Essentials: Catechism; A Guide to the Ten Commandments, the Apostles' Creed, and the Lord's Prayer* (Lexham Press, 2023).

44. These guideposts are suggested by Brad East, "Once More, Church and Culture," Mere Orthodoxy, April 18, 2023, https://mereorthodoxy.com/once-more-church-and-culture.